MW00445359

# THE P&J OYSTER COOKBOOK

# THE P&J OYSTER COOKBOOK

KIT WOHL & the
SUNSERI FAMILY

PELICAN PUBLISHING COMPANY

GRETNA 2010

Copyright © 2010
First printing, January 2010
Second printing, April 2010
Wohl & Company, Inc.
Design and Text by Kit Wohl
Photographs by Kit Wohl
unless otherwise noted.
All rights reserved
The word "Pelican" and the depiction of a pelican are trademarks
of Pelican Publishing Company, Inc., and are registered in the
U.S. Patent and Trademark Office.
ISBN 9781589806498
Edited by Gene Bourg
Printed in Singapore
Published by Pelican Publishing Company, Inc.
1000 Burmaster Street, Gretna, Louisiana 70053

# CONTENTS

In loving memory of Bobbie Sunseri

# Celebration on the Half Shell

*"As I ate the oysters with their strong taste of the sea and their faint metallic taste that the cold white wine washed away, leaving only the sea taste and the succulent texture, and as I drank their cold liquid from each shell and washed it down with the crisp taste of the wine, I lost the empty feeling and began to be happy and to make plans."*

**—Ernest Hemingway, A Moveable Feast**

In New Orleans and the rest of south Louisiana, the fresh taste of the sea that Hemingway so lovingly wrote about comes from the coastline of the Gulf of Mexico, the greatest source of oysters in North America.

Crassostrea virginica is the biologist's name for these luscious mollusks. For more than two centuries they have inspired Creole and Cajun cooks to create a multitude of mouth-watering dishes that have become legendary in such preparations as seafood gumbos, spicy jambalayas, delicately flavored gratins and soups, or lusty stuffings for fowl.

Many oyster connoisseurs claim that their flavor peak comes through when they're minimally cooked—coated with flour and flash-fried to preserve their juices, or delicately roasted with butter and seasonings, or baked on the half-shell under luscious toppings.

Others reserve their highest praise for the ones eaten immediately after they're shucked, glistening on the iridescent open shell and resting on a bed of crushed ice, ready to be gulped down along with their juices.

There was a time when finding raw oysters on a hot summer's day was difficult. That sentiment began disappearing with improvements in refrigeration, which was a boon for cooks and gastronomes, as well as for the oyster industry.

Today, in summer's hottest months, it's not uncommon for a south-Louisiana family to buy a large burlap sack filled with iced unshucked oysters, and then gather under a shade tree for a picnic, a throw-down or an old-fashioned Cajun fais-do-do to savor one of nature's greatest gifts to our taste buds.

It is in that celebratory spirit that the P&J Oyster Cookbook, with many recipes collected over many decades, led by Bobbie Sunseri of the P&J Oyster Company family, was conceived and dedicated to her memory. Her love of cooking is her delicious legacy to us all.

The Sunseri family has never lost sight of the commitment of those who went before them to produce the finest, tastiest oysters in the world.

**No institution has played a larger role in the advancement of south Louisiana's oyster industry than New Orleans' P&J Oyster Company, the oldest business of its kind in the United States.**

**For more than 130 years it has been cultivating and harvesting oysters that are consistently recognized for their uncompromising freshness and quality of flavor.**

P&J oysters were present at the creation of many legendary dishes of New Orleans' Creole cuisine. One such is the most famous oyster dish of them all—oysters Rockefeller, invented in the 1880s at Antoine's by the restaurant's proprietor, Jules Alciatore.

The story of P&J begins many thousands of miles from New Orleans—in Croatia, a region that was once part of Yugoslavia.

For the inhabitants of the Croatian villages strung along the coast of the Adriatic Sea, fishing was a way of life for thousands of years. Many generations of them also traveled throughout the Mediterranean as seafarers to practice their trade.

In the mid-1800s a large number of Croatian fishermen and their families began migrating to America. Many of them found their way to the Gulf of Mexico and Louisiana. Among these was John Popich, who settled near New Orleans. Like many of his countrymen, Popich quickly became an oyster fisherman, plying the waters of the Gulf of Mexico to cultivate and harvest the fresh shellfish that was always in high demand in the homes, restaurants and oyster saloons of New Orleans and its environs.

Popich began farming and distributing oysters in 1876. The business flourished to the point where, around the turn of the 20th century, Popich took on a younger partner, Joseph Jurisich, the orphaned son of a couple who had owned an oyster saloon in New Orleans' French Quarter. The new partnership allowed Popich to concentrate on the oyster farming operation while Jurisich focused on selling to the local market.

After a couple of years, the two men established the largest fresh-oyster business in the southern United States, P&J Oyster Company. The business prospered, and in 1921 Popich & Jurisich expanded their operations. They purchased the company's present offices in the French Quarter, at the corner of North Rampart and Toulouse Streets. They also took on a part-time salesman and bookkeeper, Alfred Sunseri, the husband of Jurisich's first cousin.

At the time, Sunseri was a full-time employee of United Fruit Company, the New Orleans-based producers of Chiquita bananas. As a salesman at United Fruit, Sunseri had made contacts in the shipping industry all over the country. These contacts allowed him to develop and expand P&J's shipping capability to the point where the company became one of the biggest shippers of gulf oysters in the southern United States. Railway Express was P&J's major mode of interstate transportation during this period. Three times a day, the railway shipper picked up barrels of super-fresh oysters—either shucked or still in the shell—from the French Quarter facility and delivered them to destinations throughout the contiguous 48 states, Canada and Mexico.

In the early 1930s Alfred Sunseri was offered a national management position at United Fruit Company if he were willing move to Baltimore, Md. He confronted the issue of his young family's financial future and accepted the promotion. Less than six months after Sunseri's departure, P&J's business declined. Popich and Jurisich realized that the workload was overwhelming without Sunseri's involvement. They contacted him in Baltimore and offered him a one-third partnership in the company. Alfred did not hesitate to return his family to their beloved New Orleans.

In 1952 Alfred's only son, Sal, began working at P&J as an accountant. Shortly thereafter both Jurisich and the elder Popich retired. In 1961, after Alfred's death, Sal Sunseri became president and general manager of P&J Oyster Company. As the years passed, Sal's partners began selling their stock to him. By the late 1970s, Sal had purchased the remaining shares of company stock and became the sole owner.

In 1980 Sal's eldest son, named for his grandfather Alfred, joined P&J. Four years later Sal's second son, Sal Sunseri, Jr., began working there. In 1991 Sal's youngest daughter, Merri Sunseri-Schneider, also joined her brothers at the family owned and operated company. Al's son Blake, a fifth-generation member of the family, has also joined the organization.

Photograph by Christopher Gromek

### Tips for Preparing
### Oysters on the Half-Shell

Whether oysters are raw or cooked, arranging them on their own bottom shells is probably the most dramatic way to serve them, especially when they're topped with sauces and garnished with herbs and seasonings.

**Serving Size**

Serving sizes for oysters on the half-shall are not specified in this cookbook because the number of individual oysters any one person will consume is completely subjective. You may be serving them as appetizers, in which case the standard number is three; or as a main course, which could mean using as few as six or as many as a dozen, or more, per serving. In the book's recipes, proportions of ingredients can be adjusted to account for varying appetites.

**Shucked or unshucked?**

When choosing oysters that are still in their shells to be served on the half-shell, look for medium-sized ones with bottom shells that have "bowls" deep enough to contain the oyster itself, as well as any topping that might be used. Another option is to buy freshly shucked oysters and obtain the bottom shells from your seafood dealer. If the shells haven't been cleaned, place them in a large pot and cover them with water. Add 1 lemon, cut in pieces, 1/2 cup of vinegar and 2 tablespoons of kosher salt. Bring to a full boil, then lower the heat. Simmer for 10 minutes, then remove the shells from the water and drain them upside down on absorbent paper, such as newspaper or brown grocery bags. We save our shells, properly sterilized, and use them repeatedly.

**The Half-Shell 'Tray'**

The most practical approach to preparing oysters on the half-shell, whether they're to be served cold or hot, is to assemble a "tray" in advance that can be used to cook them or serve them—or both. Spread a 3/4-inch bed of rock salt evenly onto a large rimmed platter or baking pan. Firmly set the shells into the salt. This not only stabilizes the shells so that they won't tip, but the salt also helps retain both heat and cold. Cover the tray with plastic wrap and store at room temperature; or, if the oysters are to be served cold, chill the tray in the refrigerator before serving. A bed of crushed ice is also elegant and keeps the oysters completely chilled. For special occasions, fancy oyster plates may add sparkle to your table. There are many kinds of glassware, tiny bowls, cups and unusual dishes available that are fun to use for serving oysters.

**Health Notice**

There may be a risk associated with consuming raw shellfish as is the case with other raw protein products. If you suffer from chronic illness of the liver, stomach or blood or have other immune disorders, you should eat these products fully cooked.

523-2651

**Oyster Liquor**

The juices found with each oyster in its shell are known as the oyster "liquor." By any name, this liquid is filled with flavor. If a recipe does not call for the liquor, always strain and refrigerate or freeze it for future use as a replacement for fish stock or when another recipe calls for more oyster liquor than you have on hand. Intensify the oyster liquor's flavor by placing it in a saucepan over medium heat and reduce it by half.

**Shucking Oysters**

First, keep in mind that oyster shucking presents certain safety hazards. Be sure to use a double-folded kitchen towel or an old oven glove to protect the hand that is holding the oyster while you're using the knife to open the shell. Special gloves and knives are available on many websites. Clean the shells by scrubbing them with a stiff wire brush under running water.

To open the oyster, insert the knife point into the "hinge" at the back of the shell until a small gap is felt. Then poke around to find the muscle that keeps the shell shut. Twist the blade firmly. Once the muscle is loosened, pry open the two shells by running the knife blade between their edges and gently twisting the blade as it's worked around the seam. Cut the attachment and discard the top shell. Cut the muscle fiber under the oyster that holds it to the shell so the oyster may be picked up with a cocktail fork.

As oysters are removed from their shells, place them in a bowl. If the oyster juices will be used in a sauce or other preparation, rid them of any stray bits of grit by straining them through a fine sieve into another bowl or saucepan. The oysters and juices should be refrigerated immediately and removed just before they're to be eaten or cooked.

Daunting? Many seafood restaurants have a staff member available for a little free-lance work either as an instructor or as your official oyster shucker. Otherwise, arrange to pick up several trays of iced and just opened oysters on the half shell from a restaurant. Of course, seafood markets sell oysters already shucked, by the pint, quart or gallon.

**How Many P&J Oysters?**

A good rule of thumb, based on the time of the year for P&J oyster count is:

1 Pint = 24 oysters

1 Quart = 48 oysters

# Raw

*An oyster fisherman in open water can grab one from the net, easily pry it from the shell and gulp it down—breakfast as the dawn breaks. But that requires a special boat drifting above an oyster bed.*

*The rest of us—for lunch or dinner—must look to oyster bars or seafood houses for a chance to savor them—just a few hours after they've been plucked from the water and trucked in from the wharf, iced down in burlap sacks. Then we can get a dozen or more, maybe with a sauce or some lemon juice, and get ready to party.*

*The deck of an oyster boat is just about as basic as possible.*

# Raw Oysters on the Half Shell

*Raw oysters on the half shell are traditionally served chilled, freshly shucked and with cocktail sauce and saltine crackers as accompaniment.*

3 lemons

cheesecloth for making 6 lemon wraps (directions at right)

crushed ice

dipping sauce*

36 shucked fresh oysters, in their bottom shells with their juices

fresh parsley sprigs, for garnish

Louisiana hot sauce, optional

*Recipes for the following dipping sauces will be found on page 213

**Red Horseradish Cocktail Sauce**

**White Horseradish Sauce**

**Mignonette Sauce**

**YIELD: 6 servings**

**Lemon Wraps**

Lemon wraps keep seeds out of the lemon juice and direct it onto the food rather than into your dinner partner's eyes. Make 6 lemon wraps by first rolling the 3 lemons on the countertop or other hard surface, pressing down with the heel of your hand to release the juices. Cut each lemon in half. Place each half, cut side down, on a 4-inch square of cheesecloth. Gather the cheesecloth up above the lemon half and tie the cloth with a bit of string.

**Assembly**

Fill each of six shallow soup plates or tin pie plates with a 3/4-inch layer of crushed ice. Position a small cup for a dipping sauce in the center of each plate and arrange 6 raw oysters in their shells around it.

Place each soup or pie plate of oysters on a large dinner plate. Garnish each serving with a lemon wrap and a sprig or two of parsley. Serve with saltine crackers and, if desired, butter pats, as well as a bottle of optional Louisiana-style hot pepper sauce.

# Oysters with Three Granités

## CHEF SCOTT BOSWELL, STELLA

*Chef Scott Boswell at Stella loves ice on oysters, which accounts for this recipe containing granités. A granité is a semi-frozen dessert of sugar, juice or water, and occasionally other flavorings. The consistency can range from grainy to that of half-melted snow. In these recipes, three different granités are used to top raw oysters on the half-shell. The optional vodkas are delicious. But vodka does not freeze solidly, so its presence will produce a slushier consistency. The recipe calls for freezing the scrubbed oyster bottom shells. The master recipe is given first.*

### DIRECTIONS FOR ASSEMBLING THE OYSTERS AND GRANITÉS

18 shucked fresh oysters, with bottom shells reserved

the 3 granités

bowfin caviar, for garnish

chopped fresh chives, for garnish

**YIELD: 6 appetizers, each composed of three oysters topped with a different granité**

Strain the oyster juices (the "liquor") into a container to remove grit and refrigerate or freeze the liquor for future use. Store the oysters and the bowfin caviar in the refrigerator to chill them well.

Clean the bottom shells completely inside and out, then place them in the freezer to get them as cold as possible before the dish is assembled.

Prepare six rimmed appetizer plates covered with beds of crushed ice and place them also in the freezer until serving time.

Place each granité mixture (from the recipes at left) in a shallow pan, then place the pan in the freezer. Allow the mixture to begin freezing, but do not let it solidify. This will require 1 hour or more, depending on the depth of the pan. Fluff the mixture with a fork every 10 minutes until the consistency reaches the point of being grainy, but the mixture still holds together.

At serving time, remove the appetizer plates and the oyster bottom shells from the freezer. Arrange 3 oysters on top of the crushed ice on each plate. Place an oyster on each shell and spoon a different granité on top of each oyster. Then top the granité with a spoonful of caviar. Sprinkle each oyster with chopped fresh chives. Serve immediately.

### CITRUS MIRLITON GRANITÉ

2 cups fresh orange juice

juice from 2 lemons

juice from 2 limes

1/2 cup finely chopped mirliton (chayote)

1 cup rice-wine vinegar

3 ounces orange vodka, optional

salt, to taste

sugar, to taste

Mix together the orange, lemon and lime juices with the chopped mirliton. Add the vinegar and optional vodka and mix thoroughly. Add the salt and sugar to balance acidity. Place the mixture in a shallow pan and follow the directions in "Directions for Assembling the Oysters and Granités" (at top left).

*(see recipes for Pickled Ginger and Cucumber Dill Granites on next page)*

*(recipes continued from previous page)*

## PICKLED GINGER GRANITÉ

1/2 cup finely chopped pickled ginger

1/2 cup finely chopped French shallots

2 cups rice-wine vinegar

1 cup pickled-ginger juice

3 ounces vodka, optional

salt and freshly ground black pepper, to taste

Mix together the pickled ginger, shallots, rice-wine vinegar, pickled ginger juice and optional vodka. Add the salt and pepper to balance acidity. Place the mixture in a shallow pan and follow the directions in "Directions for Assembling the Oysters and Granités" (previous page).

## CUCUMBER DILL GRANITÉ

1/2 cup finely chopped peeled and seeded cucumber

1/2 cup finely chopped red onion

1/2 cup chopped fresh dill

1 cup red wine vinegar

1 cup rice-wine vinegar

1/2 cup champagne vinegar

1/2 cup water

3 ounces citron vodka, optional

salt and freshly ground black pepper, to taste

sugar, to taste

Mix the cucumber, red onion and dill with the red-wine, rice-wine and champagne vinegars, and the water and optional vodka. Add the salt, pepper and sugar to balance acidity. Place the mixture in a shallow pan and follow the directions in "Directions for Assembling the Oysters and Granités" ( previous page).

# Oyster Shooters

## GAIL AND ANTHONY UGLESICH, UGLESICH'S

*You'll reach for more of these warm oyster shooters. Gail Uglesich prepared these on Martha Stewart Living's weekday television show. Anthony and Gail, his wife, presided over the famous Central City seafood haven until they closed the quirky establishment. Their son John worked with them and authored* Uglesich's Restaurant Cookbook *to great acclaim. The Uglesiches continue to be treasured friends of the P&J Oyster family. Recipe from* Uglesich's Restaurant Cookbook, *courtesy Pelican Publishing Company.*

2 cups olive oil (not extra-virgin)

1/2 cup balsamic vinegar

1/4 cup cane syrup

1 teaspoon salt

1 teaspoon ground black pepper

2 tablespoons sun-dried tomatoes, (dried, not packed in oil) minced

1/2 teaspoon dried oregano

1/2 teaspoon dried basil

1/2 teaspoon dried thyme

24 freshly shucked oysters, in their own liquor

**YIELD: 6 appetizers**

Shuck the oysters, reserving the shells. Strain the oyster juices (the "liquor") into a container to remove grit. Mix all the ingredients including the oyster juices, except the oysters, and let the marinade sit. The longer it sits, the better it gets.

Sauté oysters over medium heat in 4 batches in a 1/2 cup of the marinade for each batch, until the edges just begin to curl. Do not overcook! Place each oyster back in a shell. Drizzle a small amount of hot marinade from the pan onto each oyster. Keep warm until all batches are done.

Serve 4 oysters per person, on the half shell, or in small cocktail glasses.

Note: The extra sauce can be refrigerated and used again.

# Oysters Camille

## CHEF ROBERT BARKER

*Another way to serve chilled oysters on the half shell is found in this recipe, named for Robert's daughter Camille. The oysters are topped with a savory combination that tastes just like a spicy cocktail sauce.*

### TOMATO GRANITÉ

24 shucked fresh oysters, well chilled, with bottom shells reserved

8 Roma tomatoes, coarsely chopped

1 teaspoon worcestershire sauce

juice from 1 large lemon

Louisiana hot pepper sauce, to taste

salt, to taste

### HORSERADISH MIGNONETTE

2 tablespoons freshly grated or prepared horseradish

1 French shallot, finely chopped

1 teaspoon freshly ground black pepper

3 tablespoons olive oil

1/4 cup

champagne vinegar

salt, to taste

1 tablespoon finely chopped parsley or green onion, for garnish

crushed ice

**YIELD: 4 appetizer servings**

This part of the recipe should be done the day before preparing the mignonette sauce (below) and serving the oysters.

Strain the oyster juices (the "liquor") into a container to remove grit and refrigerate or freeze the liquor for future use. Place the whole oysters in a closed container and put them in the coldest section of the refrigerator to chill overnight. Also, scrub the oyster bottom shells clean under running water and set them aside.

A pinkish liquid is the objective in making this granité. Begin by puréeing the tomatoes in a food processor until smooth.

Rest a strainer over a medium-size bowl and line the strainer with a paper coffee filter or cheesecloth. Pour the puréed tomatoes into the lined strainer and allow the water from the purée to drip into the bowl as a pinkish, watery liquid. With your fingers, gently press down on the purée to release as much tomato water as possible. The total yield should be about 1 cup of liquid. Discard the paper filter or cheesecloth containing the pressed purée.

Add the worcestershire sauce, lemon juice, hot pepper sauce and salt to the tomato water and whisk to blend thoroughly. Pour the tomato water and seasonings into a rimmed baking pan large enough to produce a thin layer of the liquid. Cover the pan with aluminum foil and freeze the liquid until solid, scraping every 2 hours.

In a small bowl, whisk together the shallot, black pepper, olive oil, champagne vinegar and salt.

Remove the frozen granité from the freezer and rake it with a fork until it reaches a fine, snowball-like consistency.

Arrange the scrubbed oyster bottom shells on a bed of crushed ice. On each oyster place 1 tablespoon of the horseradish mignonette, then top it with 1 tablespoon of the tomato granité. Garnish with chopped parsley or green onion. Serve immediately.

# P&J's Bloody Mary Shooters

*The Bloody Mary is one of the New Orleans' most popular beverages. Oyster lovers can create the best of both possible worlds by gulping down shooters, from shot glasses or wine flutes with an oyster submerged in a Bloody Mary blend. Teetotalers can be comforted with a vodka-free Virgin Mary mix. Either way, the cold cocktail-oyster combination lends itself to any number of garnishes, such as lemon wedges, celery sticks, trimmed green onions or pickled okra. Place the glasses in the freezer for a frosty presentation.*

1 quart tomato juice

1 10 3/4 ounce can beef bouillion

juice of 1 lemon

1 teaspoon worcestershire sauce

2 teaspoons Louisiana hot sauce

1 tablespoon prepared horseradish

1/4 teaspoon celery salt

freshly ground white pepper, to taste

1 1/2 cups vodka

24 shucked fresh oysters

garnishes for 24 shooters, optional
(see suggestions in headnote)

**YIELD: 24 servings**

Mix all ingredients except the oysters in a 2-quart pitcher. Stir until well blended and refrigerate until icy cold. Fill shot glasses or wine flutes half full, add a raw oyster and garnish as desired. Serve immediately.

# P&J's Oysters with Champagne and Caviar

*This recipe allows the use of dinner plates or martini glasses for serving. (If you use martini glasses, don't forget to frost them in the freezer.) Also, any wine or liquor can serve as a creative alternative to champagne; there's no reason that vodka, tequila or a Margarita wouldn't be a fine substitution. It's a matter of your own good taste.*

*Inexpensive varieties of caviar are easily available in red, black, yellow and lime green in most specialty markets or via the Internet.*

48 shucked fresh oysters, with bottom shells reserved

2 cups champagne or vodka

crushed ice

1/2 cup chopped chives, for garnish

2 ounces caviar, for garnish, optional

**YIELD: 8 appetizers or 24 servings in martini glasses**

Strain the oyster juices (the "liquor") into a container to remove grit and refrigerate or freeze for future use.

For maximum flavor, place the oysters, champagne or vodka, chives and caviar in the refrigerator in covered containers and chill well before they're assembled.

If serving the oysters on dinner plates:

Scrub the oyster bottom shells clean under running water. Set the oysters and shells aside.

Make a bed of ice about 1/2-inch thick on each of eight plates. Nestle 6 oyster bottom shells in the ice on each plate, and place an oyster in each shell.

Top each oyster with 1 tablespoon of champagne or vodka.

If serving in martini glasses:

Place 2 oyster(s) in each glass. Top each oyster with champagne or vodka to 1/2 inch below the rim of the glass.

Sprinkle a few pieces of chopped chives on top of each oyster for color. Garnish with caviar if desired.

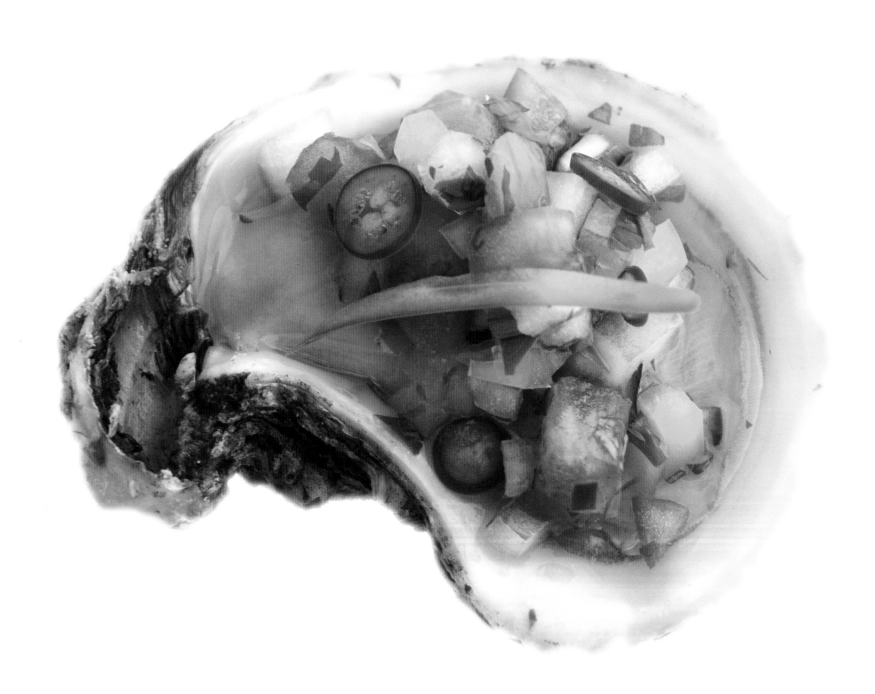

# Salsa Oysters

## CHEF SHANE BAIRD

*Ingredients from South of the Border add a lot to oysters, simply served cold as an appetizer or as a feast dressed with tortilla chips. The secret is to prepare the fresh ingredients, and cover and chill them before using them as a topping for cold raw oysters on the half-shell.*

24 shucked fresh oysters, with bottom shells reserved

the juices (liquor) from the oysters

2 cups peeled, seeded and small-diced tomatoes

1/4 cup tequila

1/2 cup fresh lime juice

1/2 cup small-diced yellow sweet pepper

1/2 cup small-diced red onion

1/4 cup finely chopped cilantro leaves

1/4 cup minced serrano chile peppers

24 paper-thin slices serrano chile pepper, for garnish

**YIELD: 6 appetizers or 4 main-course servings**

Prepare a sufficient number of half-shell trays to hold 24 oyster bottom shells, as described on page 14, using oven-proof baking pans or rimmed baking sheets.

Place one oyster on each of the bottom shells, cover and place in the refrigerator.

To peel the tomatoes, first place enough water in a pot to cover them and bring to a boil. Using a large spoon or tongs, place each tomato in the boiling water for 30-60 seconds. Remove each and run under cold water. Using a paring knife, cut the core end, and slip off the skin. Cut the tomatoes into quarters and remove the seeds under running water.

In a bowl, combine the lime juice, sweet pepper, onion, cilantro and minced serrano pepper, and chill in a covered, glass, plastic, ceramic or stainless steel bowl in the refrigerator for 30 minutes to 1 hour. When the vegetables have chilled, spoon a small mound of them on top of each cold oyster. Garnish with serrano slices and serve immediately.

# P&J's Oysters Ceviche

## SAL SUNSERI

*Ceviches are found in most Latin American countries. The typical preparation is raw fish marinated in citrus, most often lime juice. The acid in the citrus "cooks" the fish by firming it and turning it opaque. In this ceviche recipe, oysters pinch-hit for fish.*

24 shucked fresh oysters

1 ripe tomato, skinned, seeded and diced

1 onion, diced in 1/4 inch-pieces

1/4 cup finely chopped cilantro

1/2 teaspoon sugar

2 habañero or jalapeño peppers, or one of each

1/2 cup seeded and chopped sweet pepper, any color or combination of colors

1/2 teaspoon chili powder

juice of 2 limes

juice of 1 lemon

1 tablespoon minced parsley

1 teaspoon salt, or to taste

1 teaspoon pepper, or to taste

1/2 cup vinegar

1/2 cup orange juice

cilantro leaves, for garnish

lemon slices, for garnish

**YIELD: 24 oyster shooters or 4 appetizer servings**

Strain the oyster juices (the "liquor") into a container to remove grit and refrigerate or freeze the liquor for future use. Set the oysters aside.

Prepare the marinade by combining all ingredients except the oysters in a large, stainless steel, ceramic or glass bowl. Stir everything to mix the ingredients thoroughly.

Add the oysters to the marinade and cover the bowl with a lid or cloth. Refrigerate the ceviche and allow the oysters to marinate overnight.

To serve the ceviche as oyster shooters, place 1 oyster in each of 24 shot glasses or small flutes, with a proportionate amount of the marinade.

To serve the ceviche as appetizers, place 6 oysters in each of four bowls with some of the marinade and serve with toothpicks or forks. Garnish with cilantro leaves or lemon slices or both.

# Le Meritage Oyster Salad

## CHEF MICHAEL FARRELL, LeMERITAGE, MAISON DUPUY HOTEL

*This salad on the half-shell, served at Le Meritage restaurant in New Orleans, is coolly refreshing and striking to behold. The ingredients include arugula and mint in a chiffonade; that is, cut into very narrow strips as you would in preparing a julienne. Another ingredient is nuoc cham, a Vietnamese fish sauce that adds its own Asian tang to a mixture of garlic, red pepper, sugar and lime juice. The finished sauce must be prepared a day ahead.*

### LE MERITAGE SAUCE

2 teaspoons chopped garlic

1 teaspoon crushed red pepper

5 teaspoons sugar

juice of 1 lime

1/2 cup nuoc cham (Vietnamese fish sauce)

1 1/2 cups water

**YIELD: 12 small salads**

Mix all ingredients, cover and refrigerate for at least 24 hours before using.

### SALAD

12 shucked fresh oysters, with bottom shells reserved

2 cups dry white wine

2 cups water

salt and pepper, to taste

1 cup fresh arugula leaves

3 teaspoons fresh mint leaves

1 cup small-diced green, red and yellow sweet pepper

Le Meritage sauce from the previous recipe

crushed ice

Strain the oyster juices (the "liquor") into a container to remove grit and refrigerate or freeze for future use. Cover and refrigerate the oysters. Clean the oyster shells as described on page 14.

In a medium-size saucepan combine the white wine, water, salt and pepper and bring to a simmer. Add the oysters and poach them gently until the edges just begin to curl, about 1 1/2 minutes. Remove the oysters from the liquid and drain them, Pat them dry with paper towels. Discard the poaching liquid.

Begin preparing two chiffonades by first separating the arugula and mint leaves and stacking them separately on a cutting board. Roll up each stack from end to end, then slice or cut the roll-ups with kitchen shears in ribbons about 1/16 to 1/8 inch wide.

Cut the oysters into 1/2-inch pieces and mix them in a bowl with the Le Meritage sauce, arugula chiffonade (the mint chiffonade will be used later as a garnish), sweet pepper, and salt and black pepper to taste. Cover the mixture and chill it in the refrigerator.

At serving time, place a layer of crushed ice about 3/4 inch thick in the center of each of 12 small salad plates, to hold the oyster shells firmly and to keep the salad chilled. Place 2 or more heaping tablespoons of the oyster-and-sauce mixture on each bottom shell. Garnish each with some of the mint chiffonade. Serve immediately.

# Oyster Shooters

## CHEF DARIN NESBIT AND DICKIE BRENNAN, BOURBON HOUSE

*Oyster shooters are refreshing, delicious and simple to knock back. These recipes are from Dickie Brennan's Bourbon House in the New Orleans French Quarter. The restaurant contains a strikingly decorated raw-oyster bar focusing on these specialties.*

### CHAMPAGNE MIGNONETTE WITH CAVIAR

1/2 cup champagne or other sparkling wine
1 tablespoon Creole mustard
2 ounces rice vinegar
2 ounces French shallot, minced
1 tablespoon chopped parsley
salt and freshly ground black pepper to taste
1 tablespoon olive oil
24 shucked fresh raw oysters
6 ounces bowfin caviar

**YIELD: 24 servings**

Strain the oyster juices (the "liquor") into a container to remove grit and refrigerate or freeze for future use.

Whisk together all ingredients except olive oil. Slowly whisk in oil and season to taste. Place each raw oyster in a shot glass and top each with mignonette and a dollop of caviar.

### CITRUS GRANITÉ

1 ruby red grapefruit, divided into segments
1 blood orange, divided into segments
1 navel orange, divided into segments
1/2 cup citron vodka
2 teaspoons lemon zest
freshly ground black pepper, to taste
1 cup dry white wine
1 cup satsuma juice*
dash of lemon juice
freshly ground black pepper, to taste
fresh mint leaves, julienned, for garnish
24 shucked fresh oysters

Strain the oyster juices (the "liquor") into a container to remove grit and refrigerate or freeze for future use.

Cut the citrus* segments into quarters. Remove any seeds and place the quarters in a bowl with any juice. Add the vodka, black pepper and lemon zest. Stir to combine thoroughly. Refrigerate.

*Juices of other citrus, such as navel and blood oranges, can be substituted for satsuma. Create a granité by combining all ingredients and freezing them in a shallow pan.

At serving time, divide the citrus segments and juices among 24 shot glasses. Top each with a raw oyster and a teaspoon of granité. Garnish with julienned mint. Serve immediately.

### CUCUMBER AND TOBIKO

1 cup finely diced cucumber, seeds and skin removed
1/2 cup rice-wine vinegar
1/2 teaspoon chile pepper flakes
1/2 teaspoon minced chives
1/2 cup wasabi tobiko
3/4 cup seaweed salad, for garnish
24 shucked fresh oysters

Strain the oyster juices (the "liquor") into a container to remove grit and refrigerate or freeze for future use.

Place all ingredients except seaweed salad in a bowl and mix.

Divide cucumber mixture among 24 shot glasses. Top each with a raw oyster and garnish with seaweed salad. Serve immediately.

# Grilled

*Oysters may be grilled on a gas or charcoal barbecue pit or under the broiler in an oven.*

*They're a succulent treat with any method. They can even be steamed inside their closed shells or grilled on the half-shell, topped with seasonings or served with dipping sauces.*

*Once you've sampled a few of the grilled oyster recipes and tasted the various combinations of flavors, remember that seasonings can be strengthened or mellowed to your taste. You'll probably develop your own recipe.*

*Oyster beds in Louisiana's fertile wetlands, in shallow water near the shore, are leased from the state by oyster farmers, each of whom uses a different colored pole to designate his territory.*

# Grilled Oysters

## ACME SEAFOOD & OYSTER HOUSE

*Grilled oysters have been around about as long as the barbecue pit, but some New Orleans restaurants have elevated their flavor to a whole new level, and this dish is a good example. Since nature brings us the oyster already ensconced in its own pan-shaped shell, all that's necessary for grilling is opening it, discarding the top shell and cutting the muscle attaching the oyster to the bottom shell.*

1 pound salted butter

2 bunches green onions, finely chopped

20 cloves fresh garlic, puréed

1 teaspoon crushed red pepper

3 tablespoons fresh, finely chopped thyme

3 tablespoons fresh, finely chopped oregano

2 tablespoons fresh lemon juice

1 tablespoon worcestershire sauce

2 tablespoons Creole seasoning (page 219)

1/4 cup dry white wine

24 shucked fresh oysters, on the half shell

1 cup Pecorino-Romano cheese

1 loaf French bread

**YIELD: 4 servings**

A garlic butter sauce should be prepared just before grilling the oysters. Melt 1/2 pound of the butter in a large sauté pan at a medium setting. Add the green onions, garlic purée, red pepper, thyme, oregano, lemon juice, worcestershire sauce and Creole seasoning. Cook for 2 minutes.

Add the white wine and stir the mixture continuously until the green onions are soft. Remove from heat and allow to cool for 3 minutes.

Place the mixture in a large mixing bowl and add the remaining 1/2 pound of butter, which should be soft enough to blend with the sauce. Blend until the butter is folded into the other ingredients. The resulting sauce should have a creamy consistency.

Preheat the grill to 350°F.

Detach the oysters from their bottom shells by cutting the muscle beneath them. Place the oysters on the half-shell in the center of the grill. Once the juices around the oysters begin to bubble and the oysters begin to rise, ladle 1 tablespoon of the garlic butter sauce on top of each, after making sure that the sauce and its seasonings are well blended.

Top each oyster with 1/2 tablespoon of grated Pecorino-Romano cheese and allow the cheese to melt. After the oysters have browned slightly around the edges, remove them with their shells and place them on a heat-resistant platter. While the oysters are still hot, add another tablespoon of butter sauce to the top of each.

Serve immediately with warm French bread for dipping.

# Roasted Oysters with Crushed Herbs, Garlic and Chiles

## CHEFS STEPHEN STRYJEWSKI AND DONALD LINK, COCHON

*Cochon in New Orleans showcases a wood-burning oven that chefs Stephen Stryjewski and Donald Link put to delicious use. They find new ways to present traditional Cajun-country flavors in a wide range of specialties. Link has received a James Beard Award as Best Chef in the South.*

24 shucked fresh oysters, with bottom shells reserved

4 garlic cloves, minced

zest of 1 lemon

pinch of salt

1/4 cup extra-virgin olive oil

1/2 cup packed fresh basil leaves

1/2 cup packed fresh mint leaves

1/2 cup packed fresh parsley leaves

1 sprig fresh tarragon leaves

juice of 3 lemons

3 teaspoons chile paste

splash sherry vinegar

salt and freshly ground pepper, to taste

lemon wedges, for garnish

**YIELD: 4 appetizer servings or 2 main-course servings**

Strain the oyster juices (the "liquor") into a container to remove grit and refrigerate or freeze the liquor for future use. Scrub the oyster bottom shells clean under running water and set aside.

Preheat an outdoor grill or oven broiler set at high. If using an oven broiler, prepare a sufficient number of half-shell trays to hold 24 oyster bottom shells, as described on page 14, using oven-proof baking pans or rimmed baking sheets. Set aside.

Although crushing the garlic, lemon zest and herbs can be done with either a pestle or a food processor, using a mortar and pestle results in a more fragrant mixture. Using a processor involves the same number of steps but is much faster. If using a processor, be very careful not to over-process the herbs.

If using a mortar and pestle, place the garlic and lemon zest in the pestle with a pinch of salt and a few drops of olive oil. Crush into a smooth paste. Add the basil, mint, parsley and tarragon, and a few more drops of oil, and continue crushing the herbs with the mortar until the remaining bits of leaf are tiny.

Add the 1/4 cup of olive oil, the chile paste and the juice of only 2 of the lemons. Season to taste with the sherry vinegar, salt and pepper. Adjust the acid level with some of the juice from the third lemon.

Place the oysters on the bottom shells. Moisten each oyster with a few drops of olive oil and a scant pinch of sea salt, then sprinkle the crushed herbs and chiles on top of them.

If using an outdoor grill, place the oysters on the grill and cover them. If using an oven broiler, place them under the broiler. With either method, cook the oysters until they just begin to constrict and the edges begin to curl. When they are done serve them immediately, garnished with lemon wedges.

# Barbecue Oysters

## CHRISTOPHER GROMEK

*This dish was inspired by a classic New Orleans dish, barbecue shrimp. Here, the shrimp are replaced by fresh oysters, with the other ingredients remaining the same. It makes for much less messy eating, since there are no shrimp shells to remove.*

48 shucked fresh oysters, bottom shells reserved

2 cups unsalted butter

1 tablespoon worcestershire sauce

1 teaspoon Louisiana-style hot sauce

1/4 cup freshly ground black pepper

4 cloves garlic, pressed

juice from one lemon

1 teaspoon salt

1 bay leaf

1 sprig fresh rosemary

1 loaf crusty French or Italian bread

*NOTE: If you prefer even more peppery heat, double the amount of black pepper and hot sauce and add 1 tablespoon Creole seasoning (page 219).*

**YIELD: 4 servings**

Strain the oyster juices (the "liquor") into a container to remove grit and refrigerate or freeze for future use. Set the oysters aside. Scrub the oyster bottom shells clean under running water and set aside.

Preheat the oven broiler or fire up the grill according to the manufacturer's instructions.

If preparing under an oven broiler:

In a medium-size saucepan over low heat, melt the butter. Mix in all other ingredients except the oysters and the bread. When the mixture is hot, add the oysters and simmer the sauce on low heat for 2 to 3 minutes, until the oysters just begin to curl.

With a spoon, remove the oysters from the saucepan and spread them in one layer around a baking pan with a rim about 2 inches high. Then pour the sauce over them. (If you're preparing this dish ahead, it can be done to this point, and preparation can resume just before serving. Otherwise, proceed as follows.)

Place the oysters under the broiler and the bread under the pan on the lower rack to warm while the oysters cook. Watch them very carefully. When they are plump and the tops have begun to brown, remove them from the oven along with the bread.

Spoon 12 oysters into each of four soup bowls and pour the sauce over each serving of oysters. Serve immediately, along with the bread, for dipping.

If preparing on a grill:

When the grill heat reaches the point where a hand can only be held over it for only 2 or 3 seconds, it is ready.

Place an oyster on each bottom shell. Place the filled shells on the grill and top each oyster with about 1 more tablespoon of the sauce. The sauce may drip into the heat, causing the grill to smoke.

Using a brush, continue adding sauce until the oysters have curled and the sauce is brown and bubbly, which should be in 3 or 4 minutes.

Remove the filled half-shells carefully with tongs or an oven mitt and serve immediately on trays with bread.

# P&J's Garlic-Lemon Oysters

*The simple ingredients and light seasonings of this recipe allow the full flavor of the oysters to stand out. The recipe also can be adapted for outside grilling, so have fun with it. The oysters may cook faster on a grill, so keep an eye on them.*

24 shucked fresh oysters, with bottom shells reserved

1 stick unsalted butter

2 small garlic cloves, minced or pressed

1/3 cup fresh lemon juice

3/4 teaspoon salt

1 teaspoon Louisiana-style hot sauce

1 tablespoon chopped parsley or chives, for garnish

36 fresh rosemary sprigs

French bread

**YIELD: 4 to 6 servings**

Strain the oyster juices (the "liquor") into a container and refrigerate or freeze for future use. Scrub the oyster bottom shells clean under running water and set aside.

Prepare a sufficient number of half-shell trays to hold 24 oyster bottom shells, as described on page 14, using oven-proof baking pans or rimmed baking sheets. Set aside.

Preheat the oven to 425°F.

In a small skillet, melt the butter over medium-low heat. Add the garlic and cook until soft and translucent. Stir in the lemon juice, hot sauce, and salt. Lower the heat and simmer for 1 minute.

Place one oyster on each of the bottom shells and position each on the prepared half-shell tray(s). Top each oyster with an equal spoonful of the garlic-and-lemon sauce. Bake 7 minutes or until the edges of the oysters just begin to curl. Serve immediately with warm French bread.

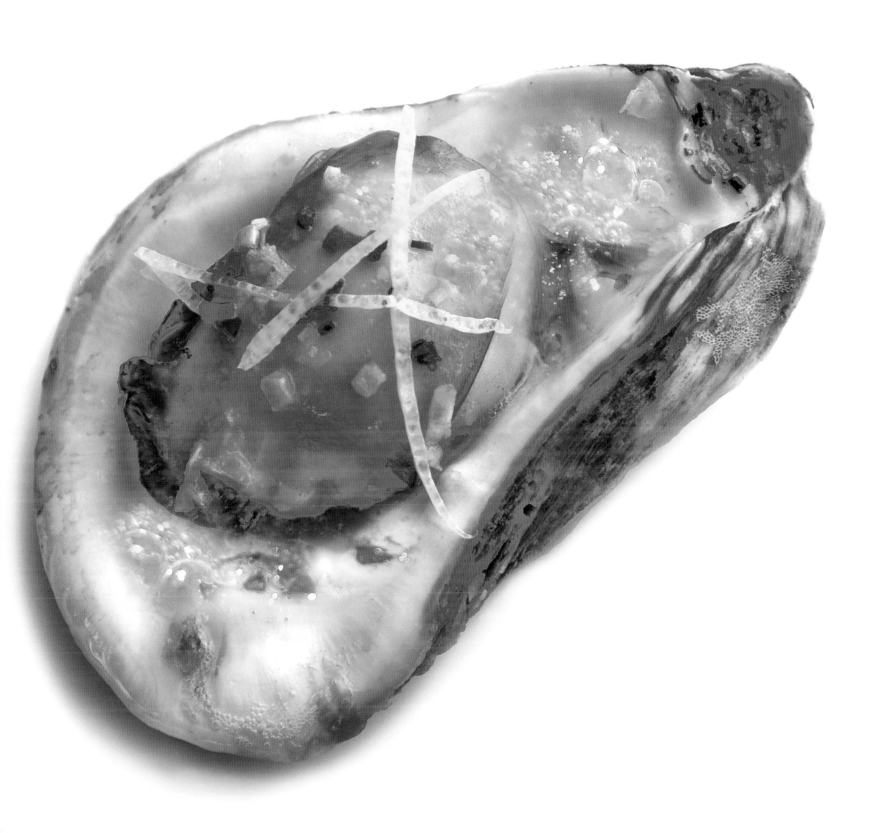

# P&J's Char-Broiled Oysters

**SAL SUNSERI**

*Sal Sunseri of P&J Oyster Company is passionate about his oysters. He's a devoted oyster lover, knowledgeable and enthusiastic. Sal's ever-evolving recipes come from the heart and are always a tasty surprise. When he char-broils oysters, this is the recipe he begins with. He then might improvise a little—or a lot—by using different cheeses, spices and herbs.*

36 shucked fresh oysters, with bottom shells reserved

1 pound (4 sticks) unsalted butter

3 garlic cloves, minced

1/2 teaspoon salt

1/2 teaspoon freshly ground black pepper

1/2 cup grated Parmigiano-Reggiano or Pecorino-Romano cheese

1 tablespoon chopped parsley

1/2 teaspoon Louisiana-style hot sauce

**YIELD: 6 appetizer servings**

Strain the oyster juices (the "liquor") into a container and refrigerate or freeze for future use. Set the oysters aside.

Scrub the oyster bottom shells clean under running water and set aside.

Prepare an open grill for direct-heat cooking. When the coals turn ash gray, they are ready.

Melt the butter in a pan and stir in the garlic, salt and black pepper. Simmer until the garlic is soft.

Place an oyster on each bottom shell and top each with some of the melted garlic butter, using either a tablespoon, a squeeze bottle or a brush. Then top each oyster with a pinch of cheese, a pinch of chopped parsley and a dash of hot sauce

Grill the oysters until they are slightly puffed up and the edges just begin to curl. Garnish each oyster with a fresh rosemary sprig and serve immediately, with French bread.

# Grilled Mexican Oysters

## LINDA ELLERBEE

*Journalist Linda Ellerbee brakes for oysters. She's a devotee, a connoisseur of most really good things. She whipped up this recipe with lush seasonings reminiscent of Mexico as a nod to Puerto Vallarta via New Orleans, when a lovely pint of fresh oysters was calling her name. The recipe is just as good whether broiled in the oven or cooked on an outdoor grill.*

24 shucked fresh oysters, with bottom shells reserved

the juices (liquor) from the oysters

3 green onions, chopped

1/3 cup finely chopped cilantro leaves

2 tablespoons olive oil

1 teaspoon ground cumin

1 jalapeño pepper, stemmed, seeded, and finely chopped

3 plum tomatoes, seeded and diced

1/4 cup tequila (optional)

**YIELD: 6 appetizers or 4 main-course servings**

Scrub the oyster bottom shells clean under running water and set aside. Strain the oyster juices (the "liquor") into a container to remove grit and refrigerate or freeze for future use.

Prepare a sufficient number of half-shell trays to hold 24 oyster bottom shells, as described on page 14, using oven-proof baking pans or rimmed baking sheets. Set aside.

Preheat the broiler or outside grill to high heat.

In a bowl, combine the green onions, cilantro, olive oil, cumin, jalapeño, tomatoes and tequila. Mix together with a fork and let stand for 30 minutes, to blend the flavors.

Place an oyster in each bottom shell and spoon some of the salsa over each, dividing it evenly. Broil on the middle rack of the oven or around the edges of the barbecue grill away from the direct heat, until the edge of the oyster begins to curl, about 5 minutes. Serve hot.

# Steamed Oysters Zach

**ZACHARY ENGEL**

*Grilling oysters is relatively simple--with delicious results. This recipe—for about 24 oysters—relies on steaming the oysters, for a different kind of treat. Get a good heat going on a grill according to the manufacturer's instructions. A hand held over the heat for two or three seconds will indicate if it's hot enough.*

*Do not shuck the oysters. Soak them in their shells in water and scrub the shells clean with a sturdy wire brush. Then scrub them again. Rinse them thoroughly while the coals are getting hot. Place the oysters, still in their shells, and with their shells' flatter sides down, directly on the grill. Cover the grill for 3 or 4 minutes. Remove the lid. The juices inside the shell should have poached or steamed the oysters. Remove them from the grill using tongs and serve them right away, still in their shells, and preferably on a newspaper-covered table. The oyster shells will have opened a bit on the grill, but they easily can be pried completely open. The trick is to insert an oyster knife or beer can opener (the old-fashioned "church key" type) into the oyster shell's rear "hinge" and twist the knife or opener.*

### NEW ORLEANS DIPPING SAUCE

8 tablespoons (1 stick) butter

2 cloves garlic, finely minced

1/2 teaspoon Louisiana-style hot sauce

1/2 teaspoon worcestershire sauce

1/2 teaspoon minced parsley

1 tablespoon Creole seasoning (page 219)

**YIELD: 1/2 cup**

In a medium-size saucepan over medium heat, melt the butter. When the butter is hot add the garlic and cook for 3 minutes. Add the hot sauce, worcestershire, parsley and Creole seasoning and then stir mixture thoroughly. Divide the sauce into two or more containers for dipping.

### ITALIAN DIPPING SAUCE

1/2 cup extra virgin olive oil

1/2 teaspoon salt

1/2 teaspoon dried oregano

1/2 teaspoon dried basil

1/2 teaspoon dried thyme

freshly ground black pepper, to taste

**YIELD: 1/2 cup**

Pour the olive oil into a mixing bowl. Add all the other ingredients and combine them well. You can also use a dried Italian herb blend instead of the oregano, basil, and thyme. Divide the sauce into two or more containers for dipping.

### SALSA DIPPING SAUCE

1 ripe tomato, 1/4-inch diced

1 small jalapeño, seeded and finely chopped

1 tablespoon minced cilantro

1/2 teaspoon salt

1 teaspoon lime juice

**YIELD: 1/2 cup**

In a mixing bowl combine the tomato, jalapeño and cilantro. Mix thoroughly and mash the mixture with a spoon against the walls of the bowl to release liquids. Add the salt and lime juice and mix well. Divide the sauce into two or more containers for dipping.

# Fried

*Next to raw oysters, there's nothing more satisfying than a pile of hot fried ones. Spread them around a split and toasted loaf of French bread, "dress" them with lettuce, tomatoes and homemade mayonnaise, and the result is a meal you won't soon forget. There's no definitive recipe for fried oysters. Each of the following recipes reflects the cook's preference for frying. Choose the one that suits your taste buds. There's an on-going battle over which is the proper batter. Some cooks prefer one containing more corn meal than flour—or no flour at all.*

*An oyster farmer's day begins early out on the water, drifting over the area he has leased from the state. Many are fourth-generation farmers, using boats that have been handed down from father to son.*

# Barbecued Oysters with Blue-Cheese Dipping Sauce
## CHEF GREGG COLLIER AND RALPH BRENNAN, THE RED FISH GRILL

*Red Fish Grill's menu gives New Orleans classics a contemporary flair that doesn't ignore Creole traditions. The dishes are served in casual surroundings that reveal Ralph Brennan's signature style – great food in a fun-filled atmosphere.*

### THE BARBECUE SAUCE

1/4 cup plus 2 tablespoons Louisiana hot pepper sauce, such as Crystal brand

1 tablespoon clover honey

6 tablespoons clarified butter (page 214)

**YIELD: 6 appetizer servings or 3 to 4 main-course servings**

Combine the pepper sauce and honey in a blender. Set aside.

In a small saucepan over medium heat, and using a frying thermometer, heat the clarified butter to 140°F. (You may also heat the butter in a microwave oven in a small microwaveable bowl.)

Promptly turn the blender to low speed and slowly add the clarified butter to the honey and pepper sauce in a thin steady stream through the hole in the blender's lid. Pour the mixture into a medium-size bowl and set aside.

### THE BLUE-CHEESE DIPPING SAUCE

4 ounces Stilton or other good-quality blue cheese, crumbled

3/4 cup mayonnaise

2 tablespoons buttermilk

2 tablespoons sour cream

1 tablespoon distilled white vinegar

1 1/2 tablespoons vegetable oil

1 tablespoon minced parsley

1/8 teaspoon salt

1/8 teaspoon freshly ground black pepper

Combine all the ingredients in a medium-size mixing bowl and thoroughly blend with a whisk. You should have about 1 1/2 cups of sauce. Transfer to a covered container and refrigerate for at least four hours or overnight to let the flavors develop, then season with salt and pepper if desired.

*(see recipe for Oysters on next page)*

*(recipe continued from previous page)*

**THE OYSTERS**

2 cups all-purpose flour

1 teaspoon Creole seasoning (page 219)

canola oil, for deep frying

36 shucked fresh oysters

barbecue sauce from previous recipe

1 cup blue-cheese dipping sauce
from previous recipe

Strain the oyster juices (the "liquor") into a container to remove grit and refrigerate or freeze for future use.

Place the flour and Creole seasoning in a large mixing bowl and blend thoroughly with a whisk or fork. Set aside.

Place a large, heavy pot or Dutch oven no more than 1/3 full of oil over high heat (or, set a deep fryer to 350°F). Set the oven temperature to 200°F. Line a baking sheet with paper towels and place it in the oven.

When the oil reaches the correct temperature, dredge the oysters, a few at a time, in the seasoned flour, shaking off the excess. Using tongs, drop each oyster in the hot oil and fry until golden, 1 to 2 minutes. Using a slotted spoon, transfer the oysters to the warm oven until all of them have been fried.

Add small batches of the oysters to the bowl of barbecue sauce and toss them to coat well. Serve hot.

At serving time, the dipping sauce may be passed at the table or presented on plates with the oysters.

# Oysters al Ajillo

## CHEF ADOLFO GARCIA, RIO MAR

*When freshly fried oysters crown French bread slices and are bathed with a tangy sauce, it can't get much better. Rio Mar in the Warehouse District happily serves these unusual appetizers.*

8 shucked fresh oysters

1 cup corn meal

1 teaspoon salt

1 teaspoon freshly ground black pepper

3 cups vegetable oil

4 slices (3/4-inch thick) toasted French bread

1/4 cup Spanish extra-virgin olive oil

2 teaspoons minced garlic

4 lemon slices

3 teaspoons chopped parsley

1/4 teaspoon paprika

salt and freshly ground black pepper, to taste

**YIELD: 4 appetizers**

Strain the oyster juices (the "liquor") into a container to remove grit and refrigerate or freeze for future use.

Toast the bread slices under the broiler or in the oven and set aside.

Place a large, heavy pot or Dutch oven no more than 1/3 full of the peanut oil over high heat (or, set a deep fryer to 350°F). Set the oven temperature to 200°F. Line a baking sheet with paper towels and place it in the oven.

Mix the corn meal with 1 teaspoon each of salt and pepper. When the oil reaches the correct temperature, dredge the oysters, a few at a time, in the seasoned corn meal, shaking off the excess. Using tongs, drop each oyster in the hot oil. Fry the oysters until golden and remove them using a slotted spoon. Transfer them to the warm oven until all of the oysters have been fried.

In a small saucepan, sauté the garlic in the olive oil over medium heat until it is soft. Add the lemon slices and a squeeze of the remaining lemon. Add the parsley, paprika, and salt and pepper to taste. Cook over medium heat for 5 minutes. Remove the lemon slices from the saucepan, using tongs.

Using appetizer-size plates, place 2 oysters on top of each slice of toasted French bread. Pour some of the sauce over each pair of oysters. Serve immediately.

# Spinach and Oyster Salad with Rosemary-Dijon Dressing

## CHEF SUSAN SPICER, BAYONA

*At Chef Susan Spicer's Bayona, she has won New Orleans' and the country's heart with her creative international take on culinary magic. She loves fresh, local products and combines them in her recipes to bring out the last bit of goodness.*

### ROSEMARY-DIJON DRESSING

2 tablespoons finely chopped French shallots

1/4 cup red-wine vinegar

1 tablespoon Dijon mustard

1 teaspoon fresh juice

1 cup extra virgin olive oil

1 tablespoon chopped fresh rosemary leaves

salt and freshly ground pepper, to taste

Louisiana-style hot sauce

### SPINACH AND OYSTER SALAD

24 shucked fresh oysters

2 cups dry bread crumbs

either 4 tablespoons chopped fresh herbs (such as sage, rosemary and parsley), or 2 tablespoons mixed dried herbs

1 cup egg whites (from about 8 large eggs), lightly beaten

6 cups stemmed, washed and dried spinach

4 large or 8 small button mushrooms, sliced

olive or vegetable oil, for frying

4 scallions, sliced thin, as garnish

**YIELD: 4 servings**

In a small bowl, whisk together the shallots, vinegar, mustard, and lemon juice. Slowly whisk in the olive oil until the dressing is creamy and emulsified. Stir in the rosemary and season with salt, pepper, and hot sauce. Taste and adjust the seasonings, adding more oil if the dressing is too sharp.

Strain the oyster juices (the "liquor") into a container to remove grit and refrigerate or freeze for future use.

Dry the oysters thoroughly on paper towels.

On a plate or pie tin, combine the bread crumbs and herbs. Dip the oysters in the frothy egg whites and then in the herbed bread crumbs. Press the oysters in the crumbs to ensure an even coating.

Lay the oysters on a tray in one layer and set aside or refrigerate (uncovered) until ready to cook.

Tear the spinach leaves into smaller pieces and divide among four plates. Arrange the mushroom slices around the spinach. Heat 1 inch of olive oil in a medium skillet over medium-high heat. Add the oysters and cook until evenly golden brown, about 4 minutes. Divide the oysters evenly among the four plates. Drizzle the salad with the dressing and sprinkle with sliced green onion. Serve immediately.

# Bacon-Crusted Oysters

## CHEF TORY McPHAIL, COMMANDER'S PALACE

*The kitchen at Commander's Palace in New Orleans is famous around the world for its deft hand at preparing all types of Louisiana seafood. Ella Brennan, who headed the restaurant's operation for more than 30 years, was awarded the 2009 Lifetime Achievement Award by the James Beard Foundation for her work in the hospitality business. "I didn't know they gave awards for having fun," she commented.*

### THE BACON BREAD CRUMBS

8 slices raw bacon

4 cups bread crumbs

5 fresh basil leaves

1 tablespoon fresh thyme leaves

salt and freshly ground black pepper, to taste

Creole seasoning (page 219), to taste

### THE FRIED OYSTERS

16 shucked fresh oysters

3 cups all-purpose flour

4 tablespoons Creole seasoning (page 219), divided

3 large eggs

1 cup whole milk

the reserved bacon bread crumbs

the reserved bacon fat

salt and freshly ground black pepper, to taste

3 basil leaves, cut into narrow strips

1 cup microgreens

1 tablespoon fresh lemon juice

1 tablespoon finely chopped preserved lemon*

4 tablespoons crumbled chetvert cheese

1 tablespoon minced chives, for garnish

*Available at specialty stores and some supermarkets.*

YIELD: 4 servings

Fry bacon strips in a skillet and drain on paper towels. Crumble into at least 1 cup of fine bacon bits. Reserve rendered fat for the second part of the recipe (below). Then, combine the bacon bits with all other ingredients in a food processor and pulse until smooth. Set aside.

Strain the oyster juices (the "liquor") into a container to remove grit and refrigerate or freeze for future use. Set the oysters aside.

In a shallow bowl, combine the flour with 3 tablespoons of the Creole seasoning and mix thoroughly. In a separate bowl, make an egg wash by beating the eggs well along with the milk and the remaining tablespoon of Creole seasoning.

Arrange the bowls containing the flour mixture, the egg mixture and the bacon bread crumbs side by side.

Pour enough bacon fat into a heavy cast-iron pot, Dutch oven or deep fryer to cover 8 of the oysters. Set the oven temperature to 200°F. Line a baking sheet with paper towels and place it in the oven.

Heat the fat over medium high heat to 350°F. While the fat is heating, dredge the oysters in the seasoned flour, using tongs, then in the egg wash and finally in the bread crumbs, shaking off any excess. When the fat reaches the correct temperature, fry the oysters in two batches of eight. With the tongs, drop each oyster in the hot fat and fry until golden and crispy, 1 to 2 minutes. Using a slotted spoon, transfer the first batch of oysters to the warm oven.

After frying the second batch of oysters, remove the first batch from the oven and immediately sprinkle all 16 of them with Creole seasoning to taste.

At serving time, arrange 4 of the oysters on each of four plates. In a small bowl, toss the basil and microgreens with the lemon juice, salt and pepper. Top each of the oysters with some of the salad. Sprinkle some of the preserved lemon on each plate. Using 1 tablespoon of chèvre for each plate, top the oysters with it, then sprinkle them with chives. Serve immediately.

# Oysters en Brochette

## GALATOIRE'S

*Galatoire's has served New Orleans locals and visitors for more than 100 years now, so it's no surprise that the restaurant is a favorite for celebrations and some of the city's benchmark dishes. Among them is oysters and bacon pieces fried on skewers, better known as oysters en brochette. The pairing of oysters and bacon delivers an amazing combination of flavors.*

18 thick slices bacon

36 shucked fresh oysters

4 wood or metal skewers (the brochettes), each 10 to 12 inches long

2 large eggs

2 cups whole milk

2 cups all-purpose flour

salt and freshly ground pepper, to taste

1 gallon vegetable oil

1 recipe meunière butter below

6 toast points

lemon wedges, for garnish

**YIELD: 6 servings**

Strain the oyster juices (the "liquor") into a container to remove grit and refrigerate or freeze for future use. Set the oysters aside.

Cut the bacon slices in half to produce 36 pieces. Cook the pieces in a skillet over medium heat for 3 to 4 minutes, to render some of the fat. (The bacon should not be crisp, but only lightly browned, and pliable enough to fold for skewering.) Drain the pieces on absorbent paper.

Onto each skewer (brochette), spear 1 folded piece of bacon, then 1 oyster. Repeat until each skewer contains 6 oysters and 6 alternating pieces of bacon. Set the brochettes aside.

In a shallow bowl, whisk the eggs and milk together to create an egg wash. Place the flour, salt and pepper in another shallow bowl or platter and mix thoroughly.

Preheat the oven to 200°F. Line a baking sheet with paper towels and place it in the oven.

Over high heat, pour enough oil to fill about 1/3 of a large, heavy pot or Dutch oven (or, set a deep fryer to 350°F).

While the oil is heating, dip the oyster-bacon brochettes into the egg wash, allowing the excess liquid to drain away. Then coat the oysters and bacon thickly with the seasoned flour, gently shaking off the excess flour.

When the oil reaches the correct temperature—or is hot but not smoking—fry the brochettes in batches, carefully dropping each one into the hot oil with tongs. Fry each batch for 4 to 5 minutes, until the oysters are golden and the brochettes float to the top. Be sure to return the oil to 350°F before frying each batch.

Using a slotted spoon, transfer the fried brochettes to the paper towels in the warm oven until all have been fried.

Remove the brochettes from the warming oven. Place a single brochette on each serving plate. Holding one end of the skewer, and using a kitchen fork, carefully push the oysters and bacon pieces to slide them off of the skewer. Place each serving of oysters and bacon on one of the toast points and drizzle generously with the meunière butter. Garnish each plate with a lemon wedge.

MEUNIÈRE BUTTER
1 stick (8 tablespoons) salted butter

1 tablespoon chopped parsley

**YIELD: 1/2 cup**

In a medium sauté pan over medium heat, melt butter until a foam appears, about 3 to 4 minutes. Once foam has appeared, add parsley and cook for 1 more minute, or until the butter starts to brown. Remove from heat and serve.

# Oysters Giovanni

## CHEF DUKE LoCICERO, CAFÉ GIOVANNI

*Chef Duke LoCicero entertains his patrons at Cafe Giovanni with extravagant dishes. The elaborate presentation of this dish offers a glimpse of his larger-than-life personality. Decorating the plate, as this recipe calls for, requires a steady hand but it's worth the effort. Using a practice plate is a good idea, and, of course, you can change the design to please yourself.*

14 shucked fresh oysters

1/4 cup sliced, unpeeled ginger

1/4 cup chopped sweet pepper

6 tablespoons olive oil, divided

1/2 cup Marsala wine

2 1/4 cup brown sugar, divided

1 1/2 cup demi-glace (page 212)

salt, to taste

freshly ground black pepper to taste

1 cup granulated sugar

3/4 cup water

1/4 cup chopped mango

1/4 cup chopped kiwifruit

1/4 cup chopped raspberries

1/2 cup dry white wine

juice of 3 lemons

1/2 cup heavy whipping cream

2 sticks butter, softened

1/2 teaspoon Creole seasoning (page 219)

1/2 teaspoon freshly ground black pepper

1 tablespoon granulated garlic

1 cup corn flour

**YIELD: 2 appetizer servings**

Strain the oyster juices (the "liquor") into a container to remove grit and refrigerate or freeze the liquor for future use. Set the oysters aside in a bowl.

First, make the ginger-pepper sauce. In a sauté pan, cook the sliced ginger and sweet pepper in 2 tablespoons of the olive oil over medium heat, until they are cooked through but not browned. Deglaze the pan with the Marsala, removing the pan from heat when adding the wine to prevent igniting the alcohol. Stir in the brown sugar and reduce the mixture until it is syrupy. Add the demi-glace and reduce the sauce by half. Strain and season the sauce to taste with salt and pepper. Set aside.

In a small saucepan, make a simple syrup by combining the granulated sugar and water and bring to a boil. Once the sugar has completely dissolved, remove the syrup from heat and refrigerate to cool.

Combine each 1/4 cup of chopped fruit with 1/4 cup of simple syrup in a blender and purée until smooth to create three accent sauces. Transfer each accent sauce into a squeeze bottle and set aside.

In another small saucepan, combine the white wine, lemon juice and whipping cream. Reduce the mixture until it is almost dry. Whisk in the softened butter. Once the butter and other ingredients are fully combined, remove the butter from heat and transfer it into another squeeze bottle.

In a shallow bowl, combine the Creole seasoning, 1/2 teaspoon of black pepper, granulated garlic and corn flour. Pour the remaining 2 to 4 tablespoons of olive oil into a skillet and to heat. Using tongs, dredge reserved oysters in the flour mixture and pan-fry them until they are crispy and golden, and the edges just begin to curl, 1 to 2 minutes. Remove the oysters from heat and drain them on paper towels.

To serve, spread half of the ginger-pepper sauce on each of 2 plates. From the squeeze bottles, swirl each of the three accent sauces and the lemon butter to form spirals from the center of each plate. Drag a toothpick across the spirals from the center of the plates to the edges, creating a pattern of broken swirls. Arrange seven fried oysters on each plate and serve immediately.

# Sweet and Spicy Sesame Oysters

## THE TASTE BUDS, ZEA ROTISSERIE AND GRILL

*The Taste Buds is the corporate name of the proprietors of Zea Rotisserie and Grill in New Orleans. They created this snappy, Asian-inspired, combination of flavors and textures, a signature of their cooking style. Their fry mixture is especially crunchy. In this recipe, they demonstrate that the addition of sauces and garnishes can make a simple recipe something special.*

36 shucked fresh oysters

3/4 cup sweet, thick Chinese soy sauce or Indonesian soy sauce (kejap manis)

2 ounces chile-garlic sauce

2/3 cup self-rising flour

2/3 cup self-rising yellow corn meal

2/3 cup self-rising white corn meal

1 tablespoon salt

1 tablespoon freshly ground black pepper

1/2 gallon (approximately) peanut oil

1 cup sweet chile sauce

1 bunch fresh basil leaves, cut into thin strips

1/4 cup toasted sesame seeds

**YIELD: 36 hors d'oeuvres, 12 appetizers or 6 main-course servings**

Strain the oyster juices (the "liquor") into a container to remove grit and refrigerate or freeze for future use. Set the oysters aside.

Combine the soy sauce with the chile-garlic sauce and mix well. Set aside. (The third sauce—the sweet chile—will not be used until serving time.)

In a small bowl, evenly combine the flour and the yellow and white corn meals and season with salt and pepper. Dredge each of the oysters in the flour mixture, lightly coating them, then gently shake them to remove excess flour. Set aside.

Place a large, heavy pot or Dutch oven no more than 1/3 full of peanut oil over high heat (or, set a deep fryer to 350°F). Set the oven temperature to 200°F. Line a baking sheet with paper towels and place it in the oven.

When the oil reaches the correct temperature, use tongs to drop each oyster in the hot oil and fry until golden. Using a slotted spoon, transfer the oysters to the warm oven until all of them have been fried.

On each serving plate, pool equal amounts of the combined soy and chile-garlic sauces. Place an oyster on each puddle of sauce. Spoon some of the sweet-chile sauce on top of each oyster. Sprinkle each oyster with some of the basil strips and sesame seeds. If serving as hors d'oeuvres or canapés, offer toothpicks.

# Mom's Fried Oysters with Horseradish Dip

**BOBBIE SUNSERI**

*The crunch of fried oysters spiked with horseradish and Creole mustard is a happy combination of texture and flavor, another Sunseri family specialty.*

### THE HORSERADISH DIP

4 tablespoons prepared horseradish

2 cups mayonnaise

2 tablespoons brown mustard

1 teaspoon dried basil

**YIELD: 6 appetizers or 4 main-course servings**

Combine all ingredients and mix thoroughly, until smooth. Place in a sealed container and refrigerate for 2 hours or longer.

### THE OYSTERS

24 shucked fresh oysters

3 large eggs

1/2 cup beer

3 tablespoons brown mustard

vegetable oil, for frying

1 cup corn meal

1 cup Zatarain's Fish-Fry or other flour mix for frying

3 tablespoons Creole seasoning (page 219)

Strain the oyster juices (the "liquor") into a container to remove grit and refrigerate or freeze for future use.

Combine the eggs, beer and mustard in a bowl and mix thoroughly. Add the oysters, turning to coat them evenly with the egg mixture. Marinate in the refrigerator for 1 hour.

In a separate, shallow bowl, combine the corn meal, Fish-Fry or other flour mix and the Creole seasoning. Mix thoroughly.

Preheat the oven to 200°F. Line a baking sheet with paper towels and place it in the oven.

Place a large, heavy pot no more than 1/3 full of oil over high heat (or, set a deep fryer to 350°F).

Transfer the marinated oysters from the refrigerator.

When the oil reaches the correct temperature—or is hot but not smoking—dredge each oyster, using tongs, in the corn meal and Fish-Fry mixture, shaking off any excess. In batches, carefully drop each oyster in the hot oil and fry until golden, 1 to 2 minutes. Using a slotted spoon, transfer the oysters to the paper towels in the warm oven until all of them have been fried.

Remove the fried oysters from the warming oven and serve immediately, with the horseradish dip on the side.

# P&J's Oysters Amandine

*Why reserve an amandine treatment only for trout? This is a take on one of New Orleans' most famous recipes. Toast the almonds in butter to release the nut-oil flavor.*

48 shucked fresh oysters

3/4 cup all-purpose flour

1/2 teaspoon Creole seasoning (page 219)

salt, to taste

12 tablespoons (1 1/2 sticks) butter

1/2 cup slivered almonds

2 garlic cloves, mashed or pressed

2/3 cup veal stock (page 212)

1 cup of the juices (liquor) from the oysters

2 tablespoons fresh lemon juice, strained

1 tablespoon worcestershire sauce

1 teaspoon sherry vinegar

peanut oil for frying

**YIELD: 4 to 6 servings**

Place the oysters and their liquor in a bowl. Holding a strainer over a large measuring cup, drain the oysters by slowly pouring them into the strainer, allowing the liquor to collect in the measuring cup. You will need 1 cup of the liquor. Any excess can be refrigerated or frozen for future use. Set the oysters and the liquor aside.

Preheat the oven to 200°F.

Place the flour, Creole seasoning and salt into a small bowl and thoroughly mix with a fork.

Melt the butter in a saucepan over medium heat. When it begins to froth, add the almonds and cook until they just barely begin to brown. Turn off the heat and remove the almonds quickly to a baking pan with a slotted spoon, allowing as much of the butter to drain off as possible. Do not remove the butter from the sauce pan. Place the baking pan in the oven.

Add 1/4 cup of the seasoned flour to the butter over low heat. Make a light-brown roux, stirring constantly. This will take about 15 to 30 minutes. When the light-brown color is reached, add the garlic and cook for 1 minute more, continuing to stir.

Carefully whisk in the veal stock and bring to a boil. Add the oyster liquor, lemon juice, Worcestershire, and sherry vinegar. Cook for 3 minutes, then remove the pan from the heat. Keep the sauce warm over slowly simmering water in the bottom half of a double boiler while you prepare the oysters.

Place a large, heavy pot or Dutch oven no more than 1/3 full of the peanut oil over high heat (or, set a deep fryer to 350°F). Set the oven to 200°F. Line a baking sheet with paper towels and place it in the oven. When the oil reaches the correct temperature, dredge the oysters, a few at a time, in the remaining seasoned flour, shaking off the excess. Using tongs, drop each oyster in the hot oil. Fry until golden, remove using a slotted spoon. Transfer them to the warm oven until all of the oysters have been fried.

Place 4 of the oysters on each appetizer plate or 6 on each main-course plate. Pour some of the sauce proportionately over each serving of oysters. Top with the toasted almonds. Serve with lemon wedges. Extra sauce can be frozen.

# Angels on Horseback

## CHEF TOM COWMAN, RESTAURANT JONATHAN

*The late, much-beloved Tom Cowman made headlines when he was chef at Restaurant Jonathan in New Orleans during the late 1970s. After that Art-Deco-style establishment closed in 1986, he eventually moved to the Upperline restaurant. This recipe was among scores of classics Cowman created during a long career in numerous other restaurants in New York City, Long Island and New Orleans.*

### MAÎTRE D'HÔTEL BUTTER

3 cups soft butter

3 tablespoons minced green onion

2 tablespoons chopped fresh basil

4 tablespoons chopped fresh chives

2 tablespoons chopped parsley

2 tablespoons chopped fresh chervil, optional

1 tablespoon onion powder

1 clove garlic, minced

1 dash worcestershire sauce, or more to taste

1 dash Louisiana-style hot sauce, or more to taste

1 tablespoon fresh lemon juice

**Yield: About 4 cups**

Combine all ingredients in a saucepan. Heat at a medium setting before serving.

This butter sauce goes well not only with fried oysters, but also with eggs, fish, meats and vegetables. For example, after pan-frying a pepper steak, put a tablespoon or so of maître d'hôtel butter in the pan with a good dash of brandy. Very carefully ignite the mixture with a match, let it flame until it burns out, and then pour it over the steak.

### FRIED OYSTERS

6 shucked fresh oysters

3 slices raw bacon

1 slice soft white bread

1/4 cup melted maître d'hôtel butter

rice flour, or seasoned flour if rice flour is not available

vegetable oil, for deep frying

1 lemon wedge, for garnish

1 parsley sprig, for garnish

Cut the bacon slices in half. Bring a pot of water to a boil. Parboil the bacon pieces in the water until they curl, about 10 minutes, then remove and cool. (This process removes excess fat and will make the bacon easier to wrap around the oyster.) Wrap each oyster with bacon and secure it with a toothpick. Refrigerate.

Preheat the oven to 350°F. Make a large crouton for each serving by cutting a 3-inch round from a slice of white bread. Brush the bread round liberally with melted maître d'hôtel butter, place it on a cookie sheet and bake it at 350°F until golden brown.

Place a heavy pot or Dutch oven no more than 1/3 full of oil over high heat (or, set a deep fryer to 350°F). Roll the bacon-wrapped oysters in rice flour, or wheat flour seasoned with salt and pepper. When the oil reaches the correct temperature, drop each oyster, using tongs, in the hot oil and fry until golden. Place the crouton on a plate and arrange the oysters on top of it. Drizzle about 1/4 cup of the melted maître d'hôtel butter onto the oysters. Garnish with a wedge of lemon and a sprig of parsley. Serve immediately.

# Oysters Benedict

## BRENNAN'S OF ROYAL STREET

*Eggs Benedict is one of the many poached-egg dishes that put the French-Quarter restaurant Brennan's on the map. A tangy hollandaise has always been the sauce often lavished on the main ingredients. In this recipe, fried oysters pinch-hit for the eggs.*

3 cups corn flour

1/2 teaspoon salt

1/2 teaspoon freshly ground black pepper

1/4 teaspoon cayenne pepper

48 shucked fresh oysters

oil for deep frying

4 tablespoons (1/2 stick) unsalted butter

16 slices Canadian bacon (preferred) or smoked ham

2 cups hollandaise sauce (page 216)

parsley for garnish

**YIELD: 8 main-course servings**

Strain the oyster juices (the "liquor") into a container to remove grit and refrigerate or freeze for future use. Set the oysters aside in a bowl.

In a shallow bowl or rimmed baking pan, thoroughly mix the corn flour with the salt, black pepper and cayenne.

Place a large, heavy pot or Dutch oven no more than 1/3 full of oil over high heat (or, set a deep fryer to 350°F). Set the oven temperature to 200°F. Line a baking sheet with paper towels and place it in the oven.

When the oil reaches the correct temperature, dredge the oysters, a few at a time, in the seasoned corn flour, shaking off the excess. Using tongs, drop each oyster in the hot oil and fry until golden. Using a slotted spoon, transfer the oysters to the warm oven until all of them have been fried.

In a separate skillet over medium heat, melt the butter and heat the Canadian bacon slices in batches. As the slices are cooked, transfer 2 of them to each of 8 serving plates, slightly overlapping the slices.

When all 16 Canadian bacon slices have been transferred to serving plates, place 6 fried oysters over the Canadian bacon on each plate and top with hollandaise. Garnish with parsley, either whole leaves or chopped.

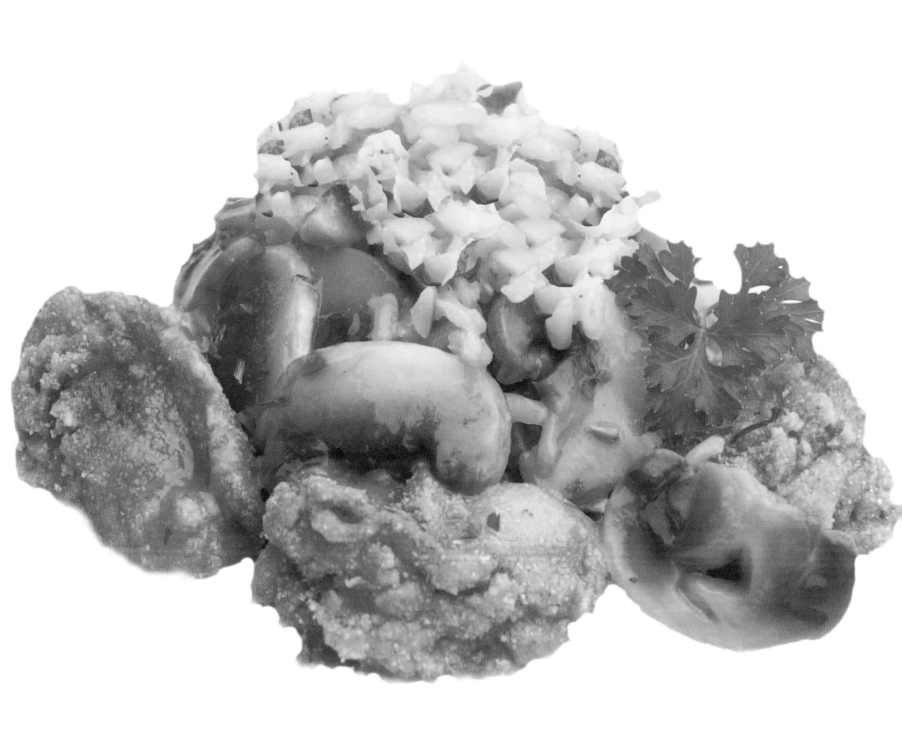

# Oysters Alvin

## WAYNE PIERCE, BON TON CAFÉ

*Founded by the Pierce family in the late 1960s, the Bon Ton Café serves authentic, more traditional Cajun cuisine from century-old family recipes. This one, handed down long ago from restaurant founder Alvin Pierce, has been updated by current proprietor Wayne Pierce, Alvin's nephew. Wayne maintains the family customs of fine food and warm hospitality.*

### SEASONED RICE

2 tablespoons unsalted butter

2 tablespoons glace de veau

1/2 cup chopped mushrooms

1/4 cup chopped yellow onions

2 cups cooked rice

salt and freshly ground pepper, to taste

**YIELD: 4 to 6 servings**

In a medium-size skillet, melt the butter, stir to incorporate glace de veau, mushrooms and onions over low flame until onions are soft, 5 to10 minutes. Stir in the rice and cover, cooking over medium heat until the rice has absorbed the liquid, about 20 minutes. Test by biting into a grain of rice. Add salt and pepper to taste. If necessary, add 1/2 cup water. Remove from heat and leave covered to continue steaming.

### ALVIN SAUCE

4 tablespoons (1/2 stick) unsalted butter

1 cup canned beef broth

juice of 1/2 lemon

1 cup sliced mushrooms

In a skillet or small stock pot over medium heat, combine the butter, beef broth, lemon juice and chopped mushrooms. Allow the mixture to simmer until slightly thickened, 5 to 10 minutes.

### THE OYSTERS

24 shucked fresh oysters

4 cups all-purpose flour

3 cups vegetable oil

1 teaspoon paprika

2 teaspoons chopped parsley

salt and freshly ground black pepper, to taste

Place a large, heavy pot or Dutch oven no more than 1/3 full of oil over high heat (or, set a deep fryer to 350°F). Set the oven temperature to 200°F. Line a baking sheet with paper towels and place it in the oven.

When the oil reaches the correct temperature, dredge the oysters, a few at a time, in the flour, shaking off the excess. Using tongs, drop each oyster in the hot oil and fry until golden. Using a slotted spoon, transfer the oysters to the warm oven until all of them have been fried.

At serving time, arrange 4 or 6 oysters around the seasoned rice on each plate. Top the oysters with a light sprinkling of paprika. Drizzle 1 tablespoon of the Alvin sauce over each group of oysters. Sprinkle each serving with chopped parsley. Serve immediately.

# P&J's Jalapeño-Stuffed Oysters

*Once a jalapeño pepper's seeds have been removed, it loses most of its heat, leaving behind a flavorful casing for oyster stuffing. This stuffing, rolled into quarter-size balls and fried, also makes a delicious half-time treat when you're cheering on your favorite team, or for a cocktail party when canapés on toothpicks are ready to enjoy.*

1/2 tablespoon vegetable oil

24 large jalapeño peppers

12 shucked fresh oysters

1 small yellow onion, chopped

1 large egg

1 1/2 cups Italian seasoned bread crumbs

juice of 1/2 lemon

1/4 cup grated Pecorino-Romano cheese

1/4 cup grated Parmigiano-Reggiano cheese

salt and ground black pepper to taste

**YIELD: 8 to 12 appetizers**

Strain the oyster juices (the "liquor") into a container to remove grit and refrigerate or freeze for future use.

Preheat the oven to 350°F.

Core the jalapeño peppers and remove their seeds. Lightly oil a medium baking dish with the vegetable oil.

Chop the oysters coarsely and, in a medium bowl, combine them with the onion, egg, bread crumbs, lemon juice, cheeses and a little salt and pepper. Mix with a fork.

Stuff the peppers with the mixture, compacting them well to ensure full stuffing. Layer the stuffed peppers in the baking dish with the tops aligned and bake for 45 minutes. Serve hot.

# Oysters Foch

## ANTOINE'S

*Oysters Foch, named for France's World War I Field Marshal Ferdinand Foch, is a staple of the menu at Antoine's, America's oldest continuously family-owned restaurant. There's no secret to the recipe, it is simply fried oysters atop toast which has been lavishly spread with duck- or goose-liver paté, then crowned with Colbert sauce. This versatile sauce, named after Frenchman Jean-Baptiste Colbert, King Louis XIV's finance minister, can be served with grilled meats, seafood and game.*

### CARAMEL COLORING

3 tablespoons granulated sugar

1 tablespoon water

pinch cream of tartar

1/4 cup boiling water

**YIELD: 6 appetizers or 24 canapés**

Put 3 tablespoons sugar and 1 tablespoon water into a small saucepan. Over low heat, dissolve the sugar, then and increase heat to medium-high. Cover and boil for 2 minutes. Remove the lid and stir in a pinch of cream of tartar. Boil uncovered until the mixture becomes very dark, about 15 minutes. Remove from heat and allow to cool partially. As it is cooling, boil 1/4 cup of water.

Add the boiling water to the saucepan and stir to blend. Cool the liquid to room temperature.

### HOLLANDAISE SAUCE

1/2 cup clarified butter (page 214)

3 tablespoons water

3 yolks from large eggs

salt and freshly ground white pepper, to taste

ice cubes, if needed

2 to 3 teaspoons fresh lemon juice, or as needed

**YIELD: 1 1/4 cups**

Warm the clarified butter. Keep it warm, but not hot.

In a small, heavy saucepan, combine the water, egg yolks and a pinch of salt. Over low heat, whisk the mixture continuously until it is foamy and thick enough to form a ribbon when the whisk is lifted above the mixture. Once the mixture has thickened, remove it from heat. If it continues to heat it will curdle. (To stop the sauce from cooking any further, you may stir in an ice cube or cool the saucepan by tipping it to the side and carefully placing the base under cold running water for a few seconds.)

Once the sauce is off the heat, begin adding the warm (not hot) clarified butter drop by drop, again whisking continuously. Add the butter very slowly for about 30 seconds, then add the rest of the butter in a very thin, steady stream, whisking until it is all incorporated.

Whisk in 2 teaspoons of lemon juice, and taste the sauce. You should be able to taste the lemon, but it should not taste sour or overpower the delicate taste of the sauce. If necessary, add more lemon juice bit by bit to achieve the perfect balance. Adjust the seasoning with salt and add a pinch of white pepper. Hold the sauce in the top of a double-boiler over warm water for up to 45 minutes. (The water must not be so hot as to cook the sauce further.)

*(See recipes for Colbert Sauce and Fried Oysters on next page)*

*(recipe continued from previous page)*

## COLBERT SAUCE

1/4 cup dry sherry

1 to 1 1/2 cups hollandaise sauce

2 tablespoons canned tomato sauce

1 tablespoon worcestershire sauce

caramel coloring

salt and freshly ground black pepper, to taste

## FRIED OYSTERS

36 shucked fresh oysters

6 tablespoons duck- or goose-liver paté
(such as paté de foie gras)

6 slices white bread

2 cups finely ground yellow corn meal

1 teaspoon salt

1 teaspoon freshly ground black pepper

vegetable oil, for frying

3 cups Colbert sauce

2 tablespoons chopped parsley, for garnish

**YIELD: 3 cups**

In a medium saucepan over medium-high heat, reduce the sherry by half. Lower the heat to medium-low and quickly stir in the hollandaise, then the tomato sauce and worcestershire. Remove from heat and add enough caramel coloring to darken the mixture to a deep chocolate color. Season with salt and pepper to taste. Set aside.

Strain the oyster juices (the "liquor") into a container to remove grit and refrigerate or freeze the liquor for future use.

Toast the bread slices and trim off the crusts. Spread 1 tablespoon of paté onto each piece of toast.

Place a large, heavy pot or Dutch oven no more than 1/3 full of oil over high heat (or, set a deep fryer to 350°F). Set the oven temperature to 200°F. Line a baking sheet with paper towels and place it in the oven.

In a shallow bowl, combine the corn meal with the salt and pepper.

When the oil reaches the correct temperature, dredge the oysters, a few at a time, in the corn meal, shaking off the excess. Then fry the oysters in batches. Using tongs, drop each oyster in the hot oil and fry until golden, 1 to 2 minutes. Using a slotted spoon, transfer each batch of oysters to the warm oven until all of them have been fried.

For appetizers, place 6 fried oysters on each slice of toast. Top the oysters with Colbert sauce. Garnish with a sprinkle of chopped parsley. Serve immediately.

For canapés, cut each slice of bread diagonally into four triangles and top with 1 oyster and some of the sauce and parsley.

# Oysters en Brochette Royale

## CHEF ANDREA APUZZO, ANDREA'S

*Chef Andrea gives oysters en brochette his personal exuberance by adding a tangy cream sauce and leeks to his recipe. His Metairie restaurant satisfies almost any yearning for an Italian meal.*

### CREAM SAUCE

1 tablespoon all-purpose flour

1/2 cup dry white wine

1/3 cup fresh lemon juice

1/4 teaspoon Louisiana hot sauce

1 teaspoon worcestershire sauce

1/2 teaspoon salt

2 cups heavy cream

### OYSTERS

24 shucked fresh oysters

24 slices pancetta or smoked bacon

1/4 cup dry white wine

1 tablespoon fresh lemon juice

1 cup water

1 fresh leek, white parts only, washed

4 wood or metal skewers (the brochettes), each 10 to 12 inches long

4 lemon wedges for garnish

---

**YIELD: 4 appetizer servings**

In a small bowl, dissolve the flour in 1 tablespoon water.

In a saucepan over medium-high heat, bring the wine and lemon juice to a boil. Add the Louisiana hot sauce and worcestershire sauce. Season with salt. Reduce heat to low and stir in the flour dissolved in water, stirring continuously.

In a separate saucepan over medium heat, reduce the cream by half. Add the reduced cream to the sauce. Keep the sauce warm in the top of a double boiler over slowly simmering water.

Preheat the oven to 400°F.

Strain the oyster juices (the "liquor") into a container to remove grit and refrigerate or freeze for future use. Set the oysters aside in a bowl.

Place the pancetta or bacon slices on a rimmed baking sheet and bake them in the oven for about 5 minutes. The slices should be pliable enough to be rolled.

Place the wine, lemon juice and water in a saucepan or skillet and bring to a simmer. Poach the oysters briefly in the liquid, until the edges just begin to curl. Remove them to a platter with a slotted spoon.

Cut the leek leaves into 48 strips, each 4 inches long. To make the strips more pliable, poach them in gently boiling water, 4 to 5 minutes. Drain them on paper towels.

Increase the oven heat to 450°F.

Lay 2 strips of leek on each slice of pancetta or bacon. Place 1 oyster on each leek-and-bacon slice near the end and roll up the slices to wrap the oyster. Slip 6 of the rolled-up oysters onto each skewer (brochette). Place the brochettes on a rimmed baking pan and bake them, turning frequently, until the bacon or pancetta is golden brown and crunchy, 12 to 14 minutes.

Set a single brochette of oysters and bacon on each appetizer plate and remove the skewer. Spoon the cream sauce over the top. Garnish with lemon wedges.

# Crispy Oyster Eggplant Napoleon

## CHEF ANTHONY SPIZALE, RIB ROOM, OMNI ROYAL ORLEANS

*The word Napoleon, used in a culinary context, usually means layers of mille-feuille pastry, cream and other sweet ingredients. The Rib Room's Chef Spizale transforms the dish into a savory main-course preparation with a terrific pairing of oysters and eggplant.*

### FRIED EGGPLANT

1 large eggplant

salt and freshly ground black pepper, to taste

1/4 cup all-purpose flour

1 egg

2 tablespoons water

1/4 cup Italian bread crumbs

vegetable oil, for deep frying

**YIELD: 4 main-course servings**

Beat the egg with the water in a shallow bowl. Place the flour in a second shallow bowl and the bread crumbs in a third. Set everything aside.

Peel the eggplant and cut it into at least 8 slices, about 1/4 inch thick. Sprinkle the slices with salt and pepper.

Place a large, heavy pot or Dutch oven no more than 1/3 full of oil over high heat (or, set a deep fryer to 350°F). Set the oven temperature to 200°F. Line a baking sheet with paper towels and place it in the oven.

Using tongs, dredge the eggplant slices in the flour, shaking off the excess. Then dip them in the beaten egg. Next, dredge them in the bread crumbs to coat them. Carefully drop each slice in the hot oil and fry until golden brown. Using a slotted spoon, transfer the slices to the paper towels in the warm oven until all of them have been fried.

### FRIED OYSTERS

24 shucked fresh oysters

juice of 1 lemon

Louisiana-style hot sauce, to taste

1 1/2 cups corn flour

2 tablespoons cornstarch

3 tablespoons salt

2 teaspoons cayenne pepper

freshly ground black pepper, to taste

1 teaspoon onion powder

1 teaspoon garlic powder

vegetable oil, for frying

4 lemon wedges, for garnish

microgreens, for garnish

Strain the oyster juices (the "liquor") into a container to remove grit and refrigerate or freeze for future use.

Place the oysters in a large bowl with the lemon juice and hot sauce marinate them for 20 minutes.

Meanwhile, in a shallow bowl, combine the corn flour, cornstarch, salt, cayenne and black peppers, along with the onion and garlic powders and mix them all thoroughly.

Place a large, heavy pot or Dutch oven no more than 1/3 full of oil over high heat (or, set a deep fryer to 350°F). Set the oven temperature to 200°F. Line a baking sheet with paper towels and place it in the oven.

Using tongs, dredge the oysters in the corn-flour mixture to coat them, shaking off the excess. Carefully drop each oyster in the hot oil and fry until golden brown. Using a slotted spoon, transfer the slices to the paper towels in the warm oven until all of them have been fried.

*(see recipe for Meuniére Sauce on next page)*

*(recipe continued from previous page)*

### MEUNIÉRE SAUCE

1 cup dry white wine

1/2 cup lemon juice

1/2 cup veal demi-glace (page 212)

4 tablespoons chopped French shallots

1 tablespoon heavy whipping cream

1 pound (4 sticks) cold butter

1 tablespoon chopped parsley

1 tablespoon chopped garlic

Divide each stick of butter into 4 pieces, each piece measuring 2 tablespoons.

Add the wine, demi-glace and shallots to a saucepan over moderate heat and reduce the mixture until the liquid is completely gone and only the shallots remain. Add the cream and combine it with the shallots. Whisk in the butter 1 piece at a time beating constantly until all the butter is absorbed into the sauce.

Strain the sauce through a fine strainer into a clean saucepan, pressing the shallots to extract their flavors. Finish the sauce with lemon juice, parsley and garlic. Keep the sauce warm, but do not allow it to boil.

### ASSEMBLING THE DISH

Remove the eggplant from the warm oven and place 1 slice on each of four dinner plates. Place 3 fried oysters on top of the eggplant slice, then a second eggplant slice on top of the layer of oysters. Top with 3 more oysters, producing a layered "napoleon" of 6 oysters and 2 eggplant slices. Drizzle some of the lemon-and-garlic meunière sauce over the oysters on each plate. Garnish with lemon wedges and microgreens. Serve immediately.

# Fried-Oyster Po-Boy

## REMOULADE

*Arnaud's little sister café, Remoulade, serves po-boy sandwiches made the way they used to be, overstuffed with plump, corn-meal-battered fried oysters on crisp, hot French bread. Arnaud's special remoulade sauce, another New Orleans secret recipe, is often slathered on the sandwich to add a tangy touch.*

2 large loaves French bread, split and toasted

1 stick softened unsalted butter

1 1/4 cups self-rising cornmeal

2 tablespoons Creole seasoning

3/4 teaspoon paprika

1 quart (about 48 fresh oysters, drained

1 quart vegetable oil for frying

1 cup mayonnaise

1/4 head fresh iceberg lettuce, shredded

2 large fresh tomatoes, sliced 1/4 inch.

dill pickle slices

2 tablespoons ketchup (optional)

1 tablespoon prepared horseradish (optional)

**YIELD: 4 to 6 servings**

Strain the oyster juices (the "liquor") into a container to remove grit and refrigerate or freeze for future use.

Split loaves of French bread lengthwise, butter each side and toast in oven. Lower temperature and keep warm.

Pour oil to a depth of 2 inches into a Dutch oven, deep skillet or fryer according to the manufacturer's directions.

Preheat heat oil to 350°F.

Mix together the cornmeal, Creole seasoning and paprika in a pie plate or flat baking dish. Coat the oysters by repeatedly tossing them in the mixture and shake off the excess cornmeal.

Using tongs or a slotted spoon, carefully place each oyster into hot oil, frying in 3 batches, 2-3 minutes or until golden. Remove carefully with tongs or slotted spoon and drain on paper towels.

Spread cut sides of toasted French bread with mayonnaise or dressings of choice.

Divide lettuce, tomatoes and oysters evenly between the French bread. Place shredded lettuce, tomatoes, dill pickle slices and oysters on bottom halves of French bread; cover with French bread tops. Slice for number of servings and serve hot immediately.

# Masa-Fried Oysters with Tabasco-Chipotle Cream Sauce

## CHEF JACK MARTINEZ AND DICKIE BRENNAN, DICKIE BRENNAN'S STEAK HOUSE

*Nothing goes better with the crunch of a just-fried oyster than a hearty sauce with a lot of kick to it. It's a bold dish not often found at an upscale steak house.*

### THE SAUCE

3 tablespoons vegetable oil

2 French shallots, sliced

6 whole black peppercorns

1 sprig fresh thyme

1 whole bay leaf

2 cups Tabasco Chipotle sauce

1 cup heavy cream

1/2 pound (2 sticks) unsalted butter

salt, to taste

### THE OYSTERS

30 shucked fresh oysters

1 bag (2.2 pounds) masa harina flour

1 cup Creole seasoning (page 219)

**YIELD: 6 servings**

In a skillet, heat the vegetable oil and sauté the shallots, peppercorns, thyme and bay leaf until the shallots soften. Add the Tabasco Chipotle sauce and reduce by half. Stir in the heavy cream and reduce by 1/3. Slowly add the butter while continuously stirring. Season to taste with salt.

Strain the oyster juices (the "liquor") into a container to remove grit and refrigerate or freeze for future use.

On a rimmed baking sheet or large plate, mix the masa harina with Creole seasoning.

Place a large, heavy pot or Dutch oven no more than 1/3 full of oil over high heat (or, set a deep fryer to 350°F). Set the oven to 200°F. Line a baking sheet with paper towels and place it in the oven.

When the oil reaches the correct temperature, dredge the oysters, a few at a time, in the crumb mixture, shaking off the excess. Using tongs, drop each oyster in the hot oil. Fry until golden, remove using a slotted spoon. Transfer them to the warm oven until all of the oysters have been fried.

Pool two tablespoons of the cream sauce on each of 6 appetizer-size plates. Place 5 fried oysters on the sauce in each plate. Drizzle another tablespoon of sauce on top of the oysters. The oysters may also be served on a platter with the sauce on the side for dipping.

# Oysters St. Claude

## CHEF KEN SMITH, UPPERLINE RESTAURANT

*Oysters St. Claude was created by Chef Ken Smith as a tribute to the great lost Mandich Restaurant that had been located on St. Claude Avenue. Upperline owner JoAnn Clevenger and Smith had a last lunch there shortly before Hurricane Katrina in 2005.*

### ST. CLAUDE SAUCE

4 seeded, thinly sliced Meyer lemons*

1 cup peeled garlic cloves

1 bunch parsley, without stems, chopped

3 tablespoons worcestershire sauce

4 tablespoons Spanish paprika

2 tablespoons Louisiana-style hot sauce

1/2 teaspoon white pepper, or to taste

12 ounces unsalted butter, melted

salt, to taste

*\*Or other thin-skinned lemons. Use peel, pulp and pith.*

**YIELD: 6 to 8 servings**

Purée all ingredients except the butter and salt in a food processor, using the metal blade, until smooth.

Add the purée to the butter in a medium-size saucepan over medium heat. Cook and stir until the garlic has softened enough to blend smoothly with the other ingredients. Be careful not to burn. The sauce will be dark red and thick. Add salt to taste. Mix the sauce well if it begins to separate.

Keep the sauce at room temperature if using it within 3 or 4 hours. Otherwise, cover and refrigerate it.

### FRIED OYSTERS

24 shucked fresh oysters

2 cups corn flour

1/2 cup all-purpose flour

1 tablespoon salt, or to taste

1 tablespoon freshly ground black pepper, or to taste

vegetable oil for deep-frying

Strain the oyster juices (the "liquor") into a container to remove grit and refrigerate or freeze for future use.

Mix the corn flour, all-purpose flour, salt and pepper in a bowl or medium-size baking pan. Dredge the oysters in the flour mixture until well coated. Shake off excess flour.

Heat the oil to 350°F. A thermometer is recommended. Do not fill the fryer more than half full of oil.

Using long tongs, place the oysters one at a time in the oil. Fry until golden brown and crispy. This should take 2 to 3 minutes. Be careful not to overcook. Remove with long tongs and drain on paper towels. Top each oyster with about 1 tablespoon of St. Claude sauce. Serve 3 to 5 oysters per person.

# Baked

Oysters Rockefeller were created at Antoine's Restaurant in New Orleans just before the turn of the 20th century. Because the dish was so rich, it was named for John D. Rockefeller, the country's wealthiest gentleman at the time. Since then, kitchens everywhere have celebrated the baked oyster. Baking oysters inspires cooks to create a multitude of toppings, fashioned from an extensive variety of ingredients and sauces.

As Miss Piggy so aptly noted, "Never eat anything you can't lift." Just about anyone can sling a sack of fresh oysters, iced in a burlap sack, into their kitchen or backyard for concoctions and creations limited only by ingredients and imagination.

# P&J's Oysters Rockefeller

## AL SUNSERI

*P&J oysters were present at the creation of many legendary dishes of New Orleans' Creole cuisine. One such is the most famous oyster dish of them all—oysters Rockefeller, invented in the 1880s at Antoine's by the restaurant's proprietor, Jules Alciatore. Al Sunseri has his own way with oysters Rockefeller. While his grandfather Alfred was a close friend of the Alciatore family, the secret recipe was never divulged.*

48 shucked fresh oysters, with bottom shells reserved

the juices (liquor) from the oysters

2 (10-ounce) packages frozen spinach, thawed

1 bunch green onions, cut into 2-inch pieces

2 celery stalks, cut into 2-inch pieces

1/4 head iceberg lettuce, cut into medium chunks

8 tablespoons (1 stick) butter

1 cup grated Pecorino-Romano cheese

1/2 cup Italian-style bread crumbs

1/4 cup anisette liqueur, such as Herbsaint or Pernod

juice from 1 lemon

salt and freshly ground black pepper, to taste

**Yield: 12 appetizers or 6 main-course servings**

Prepare a sufficient number of half-shell trays to hold 48 oyster bottom shells, as described on page 14, using oven-proof baking pans or rimmed baking sheets. Set aside.

Strain the oysters over a bowl to remove grit and to separate them from the liquor. Set the oysters and the liquor aside.

Preheat the oven to 350°F.

Squeeze as much water as possible from the thawed spinach and chop it finely.

In a food processor, pulse the green onions, celery, and lettuce until finely chopped.

In a large saucepan, heat the butter over medium-low heat. Add and sauté the chopped vegetables and spinach for about 10 minutes, stirring. Stir in the cheese and bread crumbs. (The mixture will be very thick.)

In a separate saucepan, poach the oysters in their liquor over medium-low heat until their edges just begin to curl, 3 to 4 minutes. With a slotted spoon, transfer the oysters from the saucepan to a bowl and discard the poaching liquid.

Place one oyster on each of the bottom shells on the prepared half-shell tray(s) and cover each with a spoonful of the sauce. Bake until the oysters are bubbly and the topping begins to brown, about 10 minutes. Remove the oysters from the oven and sprinkle a dash of Herbsaint and a few drops of lemon juice on top of each. Serve immediately.

# Oysters Rockefeller

## CHEF TOMMY DiGIOVANNI, ARNAUD'S

*Antoine's has never divulged their recipe for Oysters Rockefeller. The family insist that there is no spinach in their preparation, although most other Oysters Rockefeller recipes call for it. Attempts to duplicate the recipe without using spinach make use of parsley, shallots, celery tops or a combination of green vegetables. Arnaud's executive chef Tommy likes to top his with a little Brie cheese.*

36 shucked, fresh oysters, with bottom shells reserved

2 tablespoons unsalted butter

12 slices raw bacon, very finely chopped

4 cups finely chopped celery

1 cup finely chopped seeded green sweet pepper

3 tablespoons minced garlic

1 cup finely chopped white onion

4 cups blanched and drained spinach,* chopped

2 whole bay leaves

1 pinch dried thyme

1 pinch cayenne pepper

2 tablespoons finely chopped flat-leaf parsley

1/3 cup Herbsaint or Pernod anisette liqueur

1 tablespoon finely chopped fresh basil

salt and freshly ground black pepper, to taste

4 ounces Brie cheese, optional

about 2 pounds rock salt, optional

*\*Two 10 ounce packages of completely thawed frozen spinach may be substituted.*

**YIELD: 6 servings**

Prepare a sufficient number of half-shell trays to hold 36 oyster bottom shells, as described on page 14, using oven-proof baking pans or rimmed baking sheets. Set aside.

Strain the oyster juices (the "liquor") into a container to remove grit and refrigerate or freeze the liquor for future use. Scrub the oyster bottom shells clean under running water and set everything aside.

Preheat the oven to 400°F.

In a medium-size sauté pan, melt the butter over medium heat and cook the bacon until the fat has been rendered and the bacon is crisp, about 5 minutes. Add the celery, sweet pepper, garlic and onion, then stir and sauté until the vegetables are softened, 4 to 5 minutes. Add the spinach and stir for 5 minutes more. Stir in the bay leaves, thyme, cayenne and parsley, then drizzle in the anisette liqueur and continue cooking for 1 minute. Reduce the heat and simmer for 2 minutes. Remove the bay leaves, add the basil and season to taste with salt and pepper.

In a blender or food processor, purée about half of the mixture, then stir it back into the original pan, mixing together thoroughly. Transfer to a covered container, cool to room temperature and refrigerate for about 1 hour to firm the mixture.

Top each oyster with one generous tablespoon of Rockefeller sauce. If using Brie cheese, place a 1-inch square about 1/4 inch thick on top of each oyster. Bake for 15 to 18 minutes, or until nicely browned. Remove the oysters from the oven.

Carefully place 6 oysters on each warmed dinner plate. The shells will be extremely hot.

Garnish each plate with a wrapped lemon wedge and serve immediately.

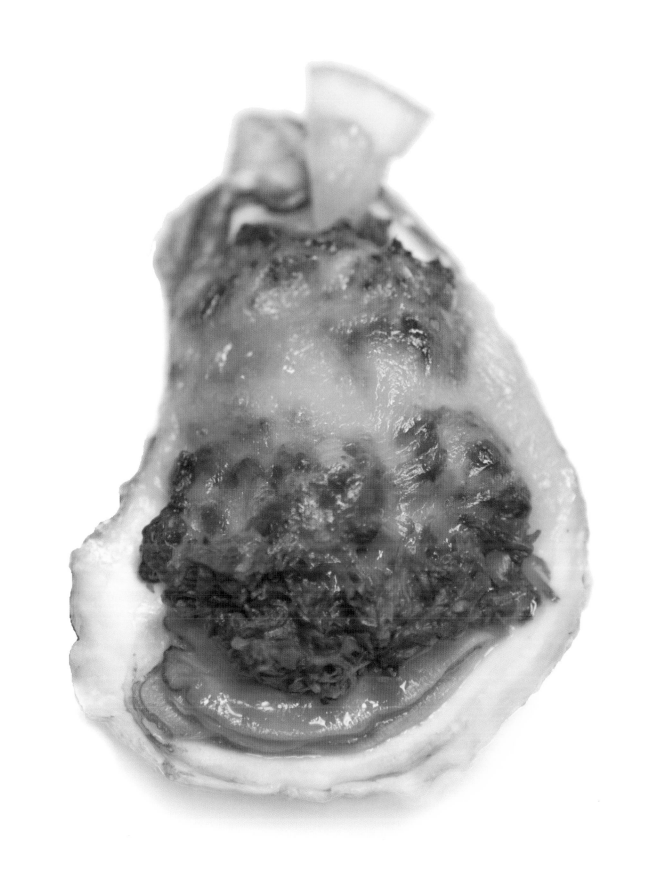

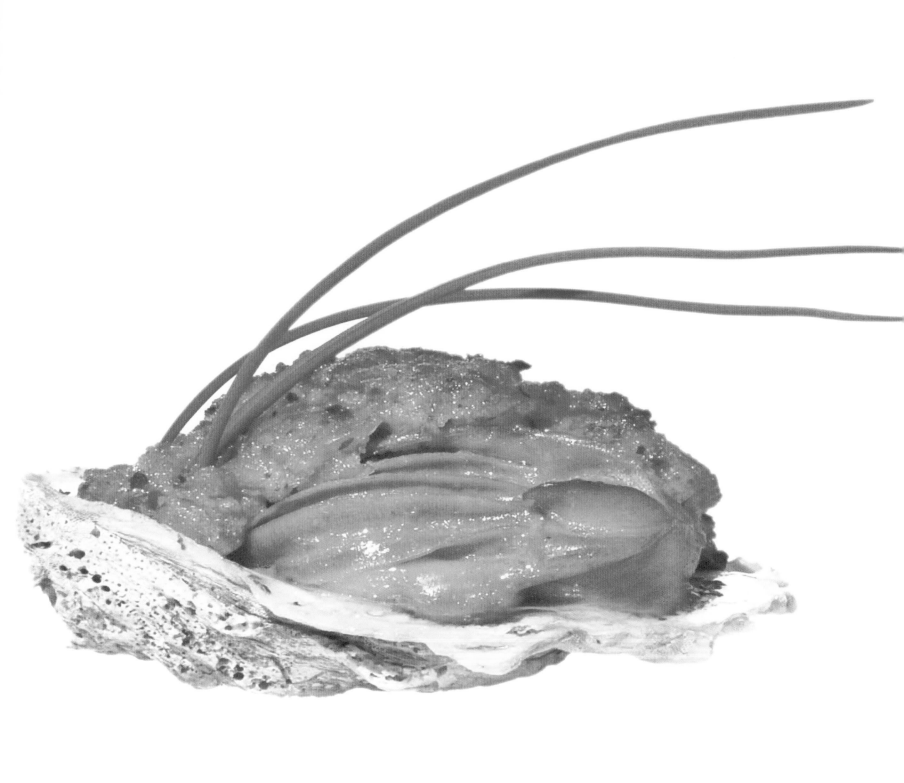

# Oysters Bienville

## ARNAUD'S

*P&J Oyster Company was the likely purveyor of oysters to Arnaud's from the time the fabled New Orleans restaurant was founded in 1918. The restaurant continues to use only P&J's fresh, raw oysters, both shucked and whole in the shell. Restaurants in New Orleans observe great loyalty to their purveyors, especially ones that have supplied them with excellent products for decades. Oysters Bienville were created at Arnaud's, and named in honor of the restaurant's location on Bienville Street.*

24 shucked fresh oysters, with bottom shells reserved

1 tablespoon vegetable oil

2/3 cup finely chopped white mushrooms

4 tablespoons (1/2 stick) unsalted butter

1 1/2 teaspoons minced garlic

4 large shallots, finely chopped

1/2 pound cooked shrimp, finely chopped

1 tablespoon all-purpose flour

1/2 cup brandy

1/2 cup heavy whipping cream

1 teaspoon freshly ground white pepper

6 tablespoons grated Pecorino-Romano cheese

4 tablespoons dry breadcrumbs

1/4 cup finely chopped flat-leaf parsley

1 teaspoon salt

freshly ground black pepper, to taste

1/2 teaspoon cayenne pepper

4 to 6 lemon wedges, for serving

**YIELD: 4 main-course servings, 6 appetizer servings**

Strain the oyster juices (the "liquor") into a container to remove grit and refrigerate or freeze for future use. Scrub the oyster bottom shells clean under running water and set aside.

Prepare a sufficient number of half-shell trays to hold 24 oyster bottom shells, as described on page 14, using oven-proof baking pans or rimmed baking sheets. Set aside.

Prepare the Bienville sauce. In a large, heavy saucepan, heat the vegetable oil and sauté the chopped mushrooms about 4 minutes, stirring. Remove the mushrooms from the pan with a slotted spoon, press them over a bowl with another spoon to remove excess liquid. Discard the liquid and set the mushrooms aside.

In the same pan, melt the butter over low heat and sauté the garlic and shallots for about

3 minutes, stirring frequently, until soft. Add the chopped shrimp and stir everything to mix thoroughly, then sprinkle with the flour evenly. Add the mushrooms, stir everything and increase the heat level to medium.

Deglaze the pan with the brandy while stirring the mixture continuously. Stir in the cream and cook for 2 to 3 minutes, until smooth. Stir in the Pecorino-Romano cheese, bread crumbs, parsley, salt, a touch of black pepper and the cayenne to a soft, moundable consistency. If the mixture is too thick, a small amount of milk may be added.

Remove the pan from the heat and transfer the Bienville sauce to a glass or ceramic bowl. Cool to room temperature, then refrigerate for about 1 1/2 hours, or until thoroughly chilled.

Preheat the oven to 400°F.

Place one oyster on each of the bottom shells and position each on the prepared half-shell tray(s). Top each oyster with 1 generous tablespoon of the Bienville sauce, compacting it slightly. Bake for 15 to 18 minutes, or until nicely browned.

The shells will be extremely hot. Carefully place 4 or 6 oysters Bienville on each dinner plate. Garnish each plate with a lemon wedge and serve immediately.

# P&J's Oysters with Pancetta

*Bacon, especially cured Italian bacon, and oysters have a special affinity for each other. The variety of herbs and seasoning makes this recipe a flavorful and colorful standout.*

24 shucked fresh oysters, with bottom shells reserved

the juices (liquor) from the oysters

24 thin strips pancetta or prosciutto

1 cup balsamic vinegar

1 cinnamon stick

4 juniper berries

2 bay leaves

9 peppercorns

8 tablespoons (1 stick) very cold unsalted butter

**YIELD: 6 appetizers or 4 main-course servings**

Strain the oyster juices (the "liquor") into a container to remove grit. Scrub the oyster bottom shells clean under running water and set aside.

Prepare a sufficient number of half-shell trays to hold 24 oyster bottom shells, as described on page 14, using oven-proof baking pans or rimmed baking sheets. Set aside.

Preheat the oven to 450°F.

Cut the stick of butter into 8 pieces.

In a medium saucepan, combine the oyster liquor, vinegar, cinnamon stick, juniper berries, bay leaves, and peppercorns. Simmer over medium heat until reduced by two thirds, about 15 minutes.

Reduce the heat to low and whisk the cold butter, 2 or 3 pieces at a time, into the oyster liquor, vinegar and spices until each piece is incorporated. If the sauce seems about to boil, remove it from the heat, to avoid separation.

As soon as all the butter has been added, remove the vinegar sauce from heat and strain into a bowl, to remove solids. Set the bowl of sauce aside.

Wrap each oyster with a single strip of pancetta or prosciutto, allowing the oyster's edges to show. Place one oyster on each of the bottom shells and position each on the prepared half-shell tray(s). Bake the oysters for 5 minutes, or until the pancetta begins to crisp.

Remove the oysters from the oven and let cool for 2 minutes. Drizzle each one with a little vinegar sauce and serve immediately.

# Oysters with Mushrooms and Aioli

## CHEF JOHN BESH, RESTAURANT AUGUST

*Silky, garlicky aioli is what gives this dish its pungent richness. It's the kind of creative touch that Besh's fans always look for at Restaurant August, or any of his growing collection of other establishments.*

24 shucked fresh oysters, with bottom shells reserved

2 tablespoons chopped garlic

2 egg yolks

2 tablespoons lemon juice

1 pinch salt

1 cup olive oil

1 cup cleaned, sliced mushrooms, wild varieties preferred

1 cup chopped raw bacon

1 tablespoon minced garlic

1 tablespoon minced French shallot

1 tablespoon fresh thyme leaves

2 tablespoons (1/4 stick) butter

salt, to taste

**YIELD: 4 servings**

Strain the oyster juices (the "liquor") into a container to remove grit and refrigerate or freeze for future use. Place the oysters in a medium-size bowl and set them aside.

Prepare a sufficient number of half-shell trays to hold 24 oyster bottom shells, as described on page 14, using oven-proof baking pans or rimmed baking sheets. Place one oyster on each of the bottom shells and position each on the prepared half-shell tray(s). Set aside.

Preheat the oven broiler to 400°F.

First make the aioli. Combine the garlic, egg yolks, lemon juice and salt in a food processor. Blend the mixture together on the highest speed. Very slowly drizzle in the olive oil into the food processor while at high speed and turn the processor off once the oil has been added and the emulsion has formed. Set aside.

In a hot sauté pan render the bacon until crisp, add the mushrooms, and cook for 5 minutes over medium-high heat, stirring frequently. Reduce to the heat to medium and add the shallot and cook 3 more minutes before adding the thyme and butter. Season to taste with salt and pepper, remove from heat.

Spoon heaping tablespoons of the bacon-mushroom mixture over each oyster on the half-shell tray(s). Add a dollop of aioli over the bacon-mushroom mixture on each oyster and broil on the middle rack of the oven until the aioli turns golden brown. Serve immediately.

# Mom's Bacon and Cheese Oysters

## BOBBIE SUNSERI

*When Bobbie Sunseri made oysters for her children, this recipe was simple to prepare and a crowd pleaser, which were the most important factors when she was serving a houseful of Sunseris.*

24 shucked fresh oysters, with bottom shells reserved

6 ounces mozzarella cheese, grated

2 slices raw bacon

2 fresh jalapeño peppers, stemmed, seeded, and finely diced

**YIELD: 4 servings**

Preheat the oven to 425°F.

Prepare a half-shell tray as described on page 14, using an oven-proof platter or rimmed baking sheet.

In a medium saute pan cook the bacon slices to a crisp. Drain them on paper towels to absorb fat. Crumble the bacon into very small pieces.

Place a raw oyster on each bottom shell. Top each oyster with about 2 tablespoons of grated mozzarella and then evenly sprinkle about 1/4 teaspoon of bacon bits and about 1/4 teaspoon of diced jalapeño.

Arrange the oysters in their shells on the tray and bake 11 minutes or until the edges of the oysters begin to curl. Serve immediately.

# Oysters Fonseca

## DICKIE BRENNAN, BOURBON HOUSE

*This full-flavored dish from Dickie Brennan's Bourbon House delivers a nice splash of color and a lot of zesty flavor. Heavy cream and grated cheese add their richness to a spectacular creation.*

24 shucked fresh oysters, with bottom shells reserved

4 tablespoons (1/2 stick) unsalted butter

2 red sweet peppers, cored and minced

2 red onions, minced

1 jalapeño pepper, seeded and minced

2 medium tomatoes, peeled, seeded and finely diced

2 tablespoons dry white wine

2 1/2 tablespoons finely chopped tasso ham

1/2 cup all-purpose flour

1/4 cup oyster juices (the liquor)

2 tablespoons heavy cream

1/4 cup grated Parmigiano-Reggiano cheese

2 teaspoons chopped fresh thyme

salt and freshly ground black pepper, to taste

cayenne pepper, to taste

2 cups French-bread crumbs

**YIELD: 4 servings**

Strain the oyster juices (the "liquor") into a measuring cup to remove grit. Reserve 1/4 cup of the liquor and refrigerate or freeze the remainder for future use. Scrub the oyster bottom shells clean under running water and set aside.

Prepare a sufficient number of half-shell trays to hold 24 oyster bottom shells, as described on page 14, using oven-proof baking pans or rimmed baking sheets. Set aside.

Preheat the oven to 375°F.

In a large skillet, heat the butter over medium heat, being careful not to let it brown. Add the sweet peppers, red onions, jalapeño pepper and diced tomatoes and sauté. When the onion and peppers are softened, deglaze the skillet with the white wine.

Add the tasso to the mixture, then stir in the flour to mix thoroughly. Cook and stir for 5 minutes. Add the 1/4 cup of oyster liquor and the cream and mix everything together again until smooth. Fold in the cheese. Season the mixture with the thyme, salt, black pepper and cayenne and transfer it to a large bowl.

Place 1 oyster on each bottom shell on the half-shell tray. Using a spoon or piping bag, top each oyster with some of the mixture and sprinkle each with some of the bread crumbs. Bake for 12 to 14 minutes, or until the bread crumbs begin to brown and the oysters are bubbly. Serve immediately, taking care not to burn yourself when transferring the hot shells to the serving plates.

# Oysters à la Provence

## CHEF CHRIS KERAGEORGIOU, LA PROVENCE

*The late Chris Kerageorgiou was beloved for his sense of fun and mastery of flavors. Shortly before his passing he sold La Provence to his protégé John Besh.*

24 shucked fresh oysters, with bottom shells reserved

2 tablespoons finely chopped parsley

2 tablespoons finely chopped garlic

1/4 cup minced French shallots

3 tablespoons sherry vinegar

5 tablespoons olive oil

salt and freshly ground black pepper, to taste

**YIELD: 4 appetizers**

Strain the oyster juices (the "liquor") into a container to remove grit and refrigerate or freeze the liquor for future use. Scrub the oyster bottom shells clean under running water and set aside.

Preheat the oven broiler.

Prepare a sufficient number of half-shell trays to hold 24 oyster bottom shells, as described on page 14, using oven-proof baking pans or rimmed baking sheets. Set aside.

Combine the parsley and garlic in a small bowl and mix thoroughly to create a persillade.

Place one oyster on each of the bottom shells in the half-shell tray(s). Season them with a little salt and pepper.

Over each oyster sprinkle approximately 1/2 teaspoon of the shallots and a big pinch of the persillade. Follow this with about 1/8 teaspoon of the vinegar and 1/4 teaspoon of olive oil for each oyster.

Place the half-shell tray(s) about 5 inches from the broiler and cook for 6 minutes, or until the oysters' edges just begin to curl and the liquid is bubbly. Remove the oysters and finish with a generous grind of black pepper on each. Serve immediately.

# P&J's Blue-Cheese Oysters

*A good blue cheese and a good baked oyster are a magnificent combination. With this recipe, any cheese you prefer can be easily substituted. It also allows you to be creative and experimental, adding dried or fresh herbs and other seasonings to the bread crumbs. Change the garnish to please yourself.*

8 shucked fresh oysters, with bottom shells reserved

1/2 cup crumbled blue cheese

1 small clove garlic, finely chopped or pushed through a press

1/4 cup fresh, seasoned bread crumbs

2 tablespoons (1/4 stick) butter, melted

1 green onion, sliced on the diagonal, for garnish, optional

**YIELD: 8 oysters on the half-shell**

Scrub the oyster bottom shells clean under running water and set aside.

Prepare a half-shell tray as described on page 14, using an oven-proof baking pan or rimmed baking sheet. Set aside.

Preheat the oven to 425°F.

In a bowl, use a fork to mix together the blue cheese, garlic, bread crumbs and butter. Stir in salt and pepper to taste.

Place one oyster on each of the 8 bottom shells and position each on the prepared half-shell tray. Top each oyster with a spoonful of the bread-crumb mixture, compacting it slightly.

Bake until bubbly, about 10 minutes. Serve immediately, topped with green onion slices if desired.

# P&J's Oysters with Baked Brie and Crab Meat

*Few oyster fans would find it easy to resist them paired with a combination of soft, silky Brie and fresh blue-crab meat. It's a feast built on delicate flavors.*

24 shucked fresh oysters,
with bottom shells reserved

2 tablespoons dry white wine

7 ounces very soft Brie cheese

12 ounces lump or claw crab meat, divided

2 tablespoons chopped chives or parsley,
for garnish

**YIELD: 6 appetizers or 4 main-course servings**

Strain the oyster juices (the "liquor") into a container to remove grit and refrigerate or freeze for future use.

Scrub the oyster bottom shells clean under running water and set aside.

Preheat the oven to 425°F.

Prepare a sufficient number of half-shell trays to hold 24 oyster bottom shells, as described on page 14, using oven-proof baking pans or rimmed baking sheets. Set aside.

In a medium-size bowl, mix the wine and cheese well with a fork.

Place one oyster on each of the bottom shells and position each shell on the prepared half-shell tray(s). Top each oyster with 1/2 ounce of crab meat. Then top the crab meat with the wine-and-cheese mixture, dividing it as evenly as possible. Press down on the toppings to compact and round them off.

Bake for 11 minutes, or until the edges of the oysters begin to curl. Carefully remove the oysters from the oven and sprinkle chives or parsley on each. Serve immediately.

# Rio Mar Baked Oysters

## CHEF ADOLFO GARCIA, RIO MAR

*The mixture of Spanish chorizo, Manchego cheese and spinach combined with seasonings, creates a wonderful baked oyster when cooked in the shell or baked in a ramekin.*

24 shucked fresh oysters

2 tablespoons olive oil

4 links (1 1/3 pounds) Spanish chorizo, ground or finely chopped

1/2 medium onion, chopped

3 tablespoons chopped garlic

1/2 cup grated Manchego cheese

1/2 cup bread crumbs

2 cups cooked spinach

salt and freshly ground black pepper, to taste

2 tablespoons butter

**YIELD: 6 servings**

Strain the oyster juices (the "liquor") into a container to remove grit and refrigerate or freeze for future use.

Preheat the oven to 400°F

In a skillet, brown the chorizo with the onion and garlic in the olive oil. Set the mixture aside and allow it to cool.

Place the cheese and bread crumbs in a bowl and mix thoroughly.

Chop the cooked spinach and mix it with 3/4 of the cheese-and-bread-crumb mixture. Add the spinach, cheese and bread crumbs to the chorizo, onion and garlic mixture, then season with salt and pepper to taste. Set the remaining 1/4 of the bread crumbs and cheese aside; this will be used as a final topping for the oysters.

Divide the final chorizo-and-spinach mixture in half. Place six 4-inch ramekins on a baking pan and half-fill each ramekin with some of first half of the mixture. Place an oyster in each ramekin. Next, cover each oyster with some of the remaining half of the chorizo-and-spinach mixture. Finally, sprinkle each ramekin with some of the reserved bread crumbs and cheese, and dot with some of the butter. Bake until the bread crumbs are golden brown, 10 to 15 minutes. Serve immediately.

# P&J's Oysters Dunbar on the Half Shell

## MERRI SUNSERI SCHNEIDER

*Merri is a cheerful soul who makes a visit to P&J Oysters as much a happy excursion as it is a joy to collect the south's finest oysters.*

24 shucked fresh oysters

12 oyster bottom shells

1 cup juices (liquor) from the oysters

2 cups artichoke hearts, cut into bite-size pieces

8 tablespoons (1 stick) butter

1/2 cup chopped yellow onion

1/4 cup chopped celery

1/4 cup chopped red sweet pepper

1/4 cup chopped yellow sweet pepper

1/4 cup minced garlic

1/4 cup all-purpose flour

2 cups heavy whipping cream

1 teaspoon worcestershire sauce

1 teaspoon Creole seasoning (page 219)

1/4 cup sliced green onions

1 tablespoon chopped fresh basil

1 teaspoon chopped fresh thyme

1/4 teaspoon ground fresh nutmeg

salt and freshly ground black pepper, to taste

Louisiana-style hot sauce, to taste

3 cups Italian bread crumbs

3/4 cup grated Parmigiano-Reggiano cheese

**YIELD: 4 appetizers or 2 main-course servings**

Strain the oyster juices (the "liquor") into a measuring container to remove grit and to produce 1 cup of liquor. Refrigerate or freeze any excess liquor for future use. Scrub the 12 oyster bottom shells clean under running water and set aside.

Prepare a sufficient number of half-shell trays to hold 12 oyster bottom shells, as described on page 14, using oven-proof baking pans or rimmed baking sheets. Set aside.

Preheat the oven to 375°F.

Chop 12 of the oysters, reserving the remaining 12 whole ones. Chop the artichoke hearts into bite-size pieces and set them aside with the oysters.

Melt the butter in a cast-iron Dutch oven over medium-high heat. Add the onion, celery, sweet peppers and garlic. Sauté the vegetables until soft, 3 to 5 minutes. Stir in the chopped oysters and artichoke hearts to combine them with the vegetable mixture. Sauté an additional 2 to 3 minutes to incorporate the flavors. Add the flour and combine everything well to create a white roux.

Stir in the heavy whipping cream and the reserved oyster liquor and blend them well into the roux mixture. The consistency should be that of a slightly-thickened white sauce. Add the worcestershire sauce, Creole seasoning, green onions, basil, thyme and nutmeg. Season lightly with salt, pepper and Tabasco sauce. Continue cooking 5 to 7 minutes.

Remove the mixture from heat and add 2 cups of the bread crumbs to it. Stir until the mixture thickens and resembles a stuffing.

Place 1 whole oyster in the center of each bottom shell on the half-shell tray(s) and top each with an equal portion of stuffing. Sprinkle some of the remaining 1 cup of bread crumbs and the grated cheese onto each oyster. Bake until the stuffing is heated thoroughly and the oysters are bubbly, approximately 30 minutes. Serve immediately.

# Baked Oysters Ralph

## CHEF CHIP FLANAGAN AND RALPH BRENNAN, RALPH'S ON THE PARK

*In a lovely old building restored by Ralph Brennan, elegantly seasoned specialties are carefully balanced for exciting tastes. From the balcony fronting Ralph's on the Park, moss-draped oak trees provide a cool vista.*

### THE SAUCE

5 tablespoons unsalted butter

1/3 cup plus 1 tablespoon all-purpose flour, divided

3 ounces (about 4 strips) finely chopped, thick-sliced bacon strips, applewood-smoked preferred

1/3 cup minced red onions

1/3 cup finely chopped sweet green peppers

1/3 cup finely chopped fresh jalapeño peppers, leaving a few seeds to add a little heat

2 whole bay leaves

1 teaspoon salt, plus to taste

1 teaspoon freshly ground black pepper, plus to taste

1 teaspoon dry thyme leaves

1/2 teaspoon crushed red pepper

2 cups whole milk

2 cups heavy cream

3 yolks from large eggs

1/3 cup peeled, seeded and chopped ripe tomatoes (or canned chopped Roma tomatoes), well drained

1/4 cup freshly grated Pecorino-Romano cheese

**YIELD: 8 to 9 appetizer servings or 5 main-course servings**

Begin making the roux by melting the butter over medium heat in a heavy 8-inch skillet. Very slowly add 1/3 cup flour, whisking constantly with a whisk until all the flour has been added and the mixture is smooth.

Reduce heat to medium-low and continue cooking the roux, whisking constantly so it doesn't scorch, until the roux turns "blond" (pale golden), 2 to 3 minutes. Set the roux aside.

In a heavy, 5-quart saucepan, cook the bacon over medium-low heat until most of the fat is rendered and the bacon is slightly crisp, about 12 minutes. Pour off all but 1 1/2 tablespoons of the rendered fat. If less than 1 1/2 tablespoons of fat was rendered from the bacon, do not add more fat to the pan.

Add to the saucepan the onions, sweet peppers and jalapeños. Cook over medium-low heat until the vegetables are cooked through, about two minutes, frequently stirring and scraping the pan bottom clean with a mixing spoon.

Reduce heat to very low and whisk in 1 tablespoon flour, mixing until well blended. Cook for 1 minute, stirring constantly. Add 1/4 cup of the reserved roux, stirring until it's blended into the mixture. Whisk in the bay leaves, 1 teaspoon salt, 1 teaspoon black pepper, and the thyme and crushed red pepper. Gradually add the milk, whisking constantly. Bring to a boil over medium heat, again whisking constantly. Reduce heat to medium-low and cook until the sauce is fairly thick, about 4 minutes, whisking frequently.

Gradually add the cream, whisking constantly, and heat the mixture until it is just short of reaching a simmer, whisking frequently. Meanwhile, place the remaining scant 1/4 cup roux in a medium-size mixing bowl. Once the sauce is close to simmering, gradually add 1/2 cup of the sauce to the roux, whisking until smooth.

Reduce heat under the sauce to very low, and add the sauce-roux mixture to the rest of the sauce in the pan, whisking thoroughly. Cook until the sauce is very thick, about 10 minutes, whisking as often as needed to keep the mixture from sticking to the pan bottom.

Meanwhile, in a small mixing bowl, whisk together the egg yolks. Once the sauce is very thick, stir about 2 tablespoons of it into the yolks, then very gradually drizzle the yolk mixture into the pan of sauce, whisking constantly and thoroughly.

*(recipe continued on next page.)*

Drain the tomatoes again and add them and the Pecorino-Romano cheese to the pan, whisking until well blended. Season lightly with kosher salt. (You may want to under-salt the sauce since you will be adding a salty cheese topping to the dish before it's baked.)

Continue cooking and whisking for one minute more. By now the sauce should be the consistency of very thick cream, leaving a distinct track on the back of a spoon when you draw a finger through it. If not, cook a little longer.

Promptly transfer the sauce to a large, heat-proof mixing bowl and resume whisking 1 to 2 minutes more.

Refrigerate the sauce, uncovered, to cool it quickly, about 20 minutes, stirring it frequently. Once the sauce is cool, discard the bay leaves. Cover and chill until it's the consistency of a thick pudding, at least 1 hour or overnight.

**FINISHING THE DISH**

Prepare a sufficient number of half-shell trays to hold 24 oyster bottom shells, as described on page 14, using oven-proof baking pans or rimmed baking sheets. Set aside.

Strain the oyster juices (the "liquor") into a container to remove grit and refrigerate or freeze for future use. Scrub the oyster bottom shells clean under running water and set aside.

In a heavy 12-inch skillet, melt the butter over medium-high heat. Add the spinach and turn with tongs to coat all the leaves with butter. Season with a little salt and pepper and cook until just barely done.

Immediately spread the spinach out on a platter so it won't continue cooking by residual heat. Once the spinach is cool, drain in a mesh strainer, lightly pressing to extract as much liquid as possible. Place in a bowl and set aside.

For the topping, combine the breadcrumbs and Romano cheese. Set aside.

Preheat the oven to 475°F. If cooking all the oysters on the same baking sheet, place an oven rack in the middle of the oven before preheating it, for safety reasons. If cooking them on two different oven racks, position the two racks in the middle third of the oven before preheating it.

Remove the chilled sauce from the refrigerator.

Position each bottom shell on the prepared half-shell tray(s) and place 1 rounded tablespoon of the spinach on each of the shells. Next, arrange an oyster on top of each mound of spinach. Sprinkle 1/2 teaspoon of the bread-crumb topping over each oyster. Spread 1 rounded tablespoon of sauce completely over the oyster to coat it with a 1/4-inch-thick layer of sauce, sealing the oyster between the sauce and the shell. Now, sprinkle an additional 1/2 teaspoon of bread-crumb topping over the sauce on each oyster.

Bake uncovered until the topping is light golden brown and the liquid is bubbling, about 12 minutes. Serve piping hot.

# Grand Oysters

## CHEF MARK FALGOUST AND JOEL DONDIS , GRAND ISLE RESTAURANT

*Joel Dondis and Chef Mark Falgoust, have added tasso and jalapeño pepper to their signature oyster recipe, creating a balance of spicy and salty. Dondis operates a group of food-related businesses that also includes La Petite Grocery, Sucré and Joel's Fine Catering.*

24 shucked fresh oysters, with bottom shells reserved

8 tablespoons (1 stick) butter

1/2 cup minced yellow onion

1/4 minced garlic

1/2 cup minced green sweet pepper

1/4 cup finely diced tasso ham

1/2 cup minced celery

1/4 cup chopped parsley

1 cup bread crumbs

1/2 cup chopped green onions

1 cup grated Parmigiano-Reggiano cheese

1/2 cup minced jalapeño pepper

1 cup shredded Monterey Jack cheese

**YIELD: 6 appetizers**

Preheat the oven to 500°F.

Strain the oyster juices (the "liquor") into a container to remove grit and refrigerate or freeze the liquor for future use. Scrub the oyster bottom shells clean under running water.

Prepare a sufficient number of half-shell trays to hold 24 oyster bottom shells, as described on page 14, using oven-proof baking pans or rimmed baking sheets. Set aside.

Heat the butter in a large skillet and sauté in it the onion, garlic, sweet pepper and tasso ham for 3 minutes, or until the vegetables are softened. Set aside.

In a large bowl, combine the celery, parsley, bread crumbs, green onions, jalapeño pepper and the two cheeses. Transfer the vegetables and tasso ham from the skillet to the bowl and combine the two, mixing thoroughly.

Place one oyster on each of the bottom shells and position each on the prepared half-shell tray(s). Top each oyster with 1 tablespoon of the mixture, compacting it slightly. Bake until the topping becomes bubbly and the oysters' edges begin to curl, about 10 minutes. Serve immediately.

# Oyster Pan Roast

## CHEF DARIN NESBIT AND DICKIE BRENNAN, PALACE CAFÉ

*At Palace Café, siblings Dickie Brennan and Lauren Brower have staffed a kitchen that revitalizes old Creole classics and creates new ones. The Canal Street restaurant, at the edge of the French Quarter, is a companion to Dickie and Lauren's other New Orleans establishments, Bourbon House and Dickie Brennan's Steak House.*

4 slices French bread, cut on a bias, 2 to 3 inches thick

1 tablespoon butter, softened

salt and freshly ground white pepper, to taste

4 tablespoons bread crumbs

2 tablespoons freshly grated Parmigiano-Reggiano cheese

1 quart heavy cream

1 tablespoon minced fresh rosemary

1 tablespoon minced French shallots

20 shucked fresh oysters

1 tablespoon finely chopped parsley, for garnish

4 sprigs fresh rosemary

**YIELD: 4 servings**

Strain the oyster juices (the "liquor") into a container to remove grit and refrigerate or freeze for future use.

Preheat the oven to 350°F.

To make croutons, butter both sides of each slice of French bread and season it with salt and white pepper. Toast the slices in the oven until crisp.

Mix the bread crumbs and Parmigiano-Reggiano cheese in a small bowl and set aside.

In a heavy saucepan over medium-high heat, reduce the cream by half. Stir in the rosemary and shallots and reduce the sauce until it thickens a bit.

Strain the sauce into an oven-proof skillet, removing the shallots and rosemary. Bring to a boil. Add the oysters and season to taste with salt and white pepper. Be careful not to over-salt the dish. Remember, the oysters are somewhat salty. Cook for 1 to 2 minutes, or until the edges of the oysters begin to curl, then remove from heat.

Sprinkle the bread crumbs and Parmigiano-Reggiano cheese over the oysters. Broil in a 350°F oven until the bread crumbs are toasted and golden brown.

To serve, place a crouton in the center of each serving plate. Spoon the oysters and sauce around the crouton. Spear a rosemary sprig through each crouton and sprinkle each serving with parsley.

# Baked Oysters with Asparagus and Crab Meat

## CHEF FRANK BRIGTSEN, BRIGTSEN'S

*After working with legendary Chef Paul Prudhomme, Frank Brigtsen opened his namesake restaurant with his wife Marna in a quaint uptown cottage where his elegantly redefined south-Louisiana cuisine is the star. The James Beard Foundation has awarded Frank the title of Best Chef in the Southern region.*

30 shucked fresh oysters, with bottom shells reserved

the juices (liquor) from the oysters

2 tablespoons unsalted butter

1 cup (1/2 pound) lump crab meat, picked over for shells

1/2 teaspoon Chef Paul Prudhomme's Seafood Magic seasoning

1/2 teaspoon worcestershire sauce

3 bunches (30 spears) fresh green asparagus, standard size, woody ends snapped off

1 tablespoon sea salt

1/2 teaspoon freshly ground white pepper

2 tablespoons fresh-squeezed lemon juice

1 cup extra-virgin olive oil

1/2 cup finely grated Parmigiano-Reggiano cheese

1 cup plain French bread crumbs

**YIELD: 6 appetizers**

Strain the oyster juices (the "liquor") into a bowl to remove grit. Place the whole oysters in a separate bowl. Set aside both the oysters and the liquor. Scrub the oyster bottom shells clean under running water and set aside.

Prepare or a sufficient number of trays to hold 30 oyster bottom shells, as described on page 14, using oven-proof baking pans or rimmed baking sheets.

In a large skillet, melt the butter over medium-high heat. Add the crab meat, Seafood Magic seasoning and worcestershire sauce. Cook for 2 to 3 minutes, stirring occasionally, until the crab meat is heated through. Transfer the mixture to a shallow pan and refrigerate until fully chilled.

Fill a large bowl with cold water and ice and set aside. Bring a large pot of water to a boil. Peel the bottom 2 inches of the asparagus spears with a vegetable peeler. Place all of the asparagus in boiling water and blanch for 1 to 2 minutes, depending on their thickness. Remove the asparagus and plunge the spears quickly into the ice water.

Remove the asparagus from the iced water and trim 1 1/2 inch off the top of each spear. Set the trimmed pieces aside for use as a final garnish.

Thinly slice (1/8 inch) enough of the asparagus stems to yield 1 cup of slices. Set these aside also.

Preheat oven to 500°F.

Roughly chop the remaining asparagus stems and transfer them to a food processor. Add the reserved strained oyster liquor, the sea salt, white pepper and lemon juice. Pulse on and off until the mixture forms a thick purée. With the food processor running, slowly add the olive oil until the mixture emulsifies.

Transfer the asparagus purée to a mixing bowl and fold in the chilled crab meat, thinly sliced asparagus, grated cheese and bread crumbs, until the mixture is evenly blended.

Place one oyster on each of the 30 bottom shells and position each on the prepared half-shell trays.

Top each oyster with about 2 tablespoons of the asparagus mixture. Split the reserved asparagus tips in half lengthwise and criss-cross the two pieces on top of each oyster, with the cut sides up.

Bake 5 to 10 minutes, or until bubbly. Serve immediately.

# Oysters Carnival

## CHEF WARREN LERUTH, LERUTH'S

*This is one of many classic creations that once graced the tables at LeRuth's, founded by the late, legendary New Orleans chef Warren LeRuth.*

48 shucked fresh oysters

the juices (liquor) from the oysters

36 oyster bottom shells

18 strips raw bacon

5 cups minced onions

1/2 tablespoon minced garlic

1 bay leaf, minced

4 celery stalks, minced

1/2 teaspoon fresh thyme leaves

10 tablespoons butter, divided

1 1/2 cups bread crumbs

6 lemon wedges, for garnish

**YIELD: 12 appetizers or 6 main-course servings**

Strain the oyster juices (the "liquor") into a measuring container to produce 1 cup of liquor. Set aside the 1 cup of liquor and the whole oysters. Scrub 36 of the oyster shells clean under running water and set them aside.

Prepare a sufficient number of half-shell trays to hold the 36 oyster bottom shells, as described on page 14, using oven-proof baking pans or rimmed baking sheets. Set aside.

Chop the oysters coarsely. Cook the bacon strips until they are just crisp. They should not be brittle or overcooked. Drain the bacon on paper towels, then cut each strip in half and set them aside.

Preheat the oven to 375°F.

Melt 6 tablespoons of the butter in iron skillet and sauté the onions, garlic, bay leaf, celery and thyme for about 15 minutes. Add the chopped oysters. Moisten 1 cup of the bread crumbs with about 1 cup of the oyster liquor and add the mixture to the skillet. Simmer for 20 to 30 minutes. Add the remaining 4 tablespoons of butter and stir until the butter is melted. Remove from heat.

Place 1 oyster on each of the bottom shells on the prepared half-shell tray(s). Top each oyster with a spoonful of the chopped-oysters-and-bread-crumb mixture, compacting the topping slightly. Sprinkle the remaining 1/2 cup of bread crumbs over the tops. Garnish the top of each oyster further with a half-strip of bacon. Bake for 10 to 15 minutes or until the oysters are heated through and the filling is bubbly, 10 to 15 minutes. Serve immediately, with

# Oyster-Stuffed Potatoes

## CHEF LEAH CHASE, DOOKY CHASE'S

*Leah Chase, widely considered "the queen of Creole cuisine," and fellow chef John Folse brainstormed this as an appetizer for a special event. The potato shells are hollowed out, then stuffed with oysters, seasonings, mashed potato and bread crumbs. Folse says that every plate Leah serves contains a bit of Creole culture being preserved. With a heart as wide as her smile, she has served nothing but P&J oysters since she began cooking in the family restaurant 65 years ago.*

6 whole medium red potatoes, preferably oblong

24 shucked fresh oysters, chopped

the juices (liquor) from the oysters

1 tablespoon butter

1/4 cup chopped green onion

4 garlic cloves, mashed or pressed, chopped

1/4 teaspoon Lawry's Seasoned Salt

freshly ground black pepper, to taste

1 tablespoon chopped parsley

1/4 cup bread crumbs

paprika, for garnish

**YIELD: 4 to 6 servings**

Strain the oyster juices (liquor) to remove grit and reserve the liquor. Chop the oysters coarsely and set them aside with the strained liquor.

Scrub the potatoes, and do not peel them. Carefully drop the potatoes, still in their skins, into a pot of boiling water. Cook until the potatoes are just tender, about 15 minutes. Let them cool, then cut them in half lengthwise.

Preheat the oven to 375°F.

Scoop out just enough of the flesh from the potato halves to keep the "shells" intact, and set everything aside.

Place the oysters in a saucepan with all of the reserved oyster liquor. Over medium heat, bring the liquid to a simmer and cook until the oysters just begin to curl at the edges, about 10 minutes. With a slotted spoon, remove the oysters from the saucepan into a bowl and pour the liquor into a separate small bowl. Set the oysters and liquor aside.

Heat the butter in a skillet. Add the green onion and garlic, and cook about 10 minutes over medium-low heat, being careful not to burn the vegetables. Add the chopped oysters to the green onion and garlic, and stir well. Stir in the reserved oyster liquor and cook 5 minutes.

Mash the reserved potato flesh and add it to the oyster mixture. Season the mixture with the seasoned salt and the black pepper. Stir in the parsley and mix everything well. With a small spoon, fill each potato shell with some of the potato-oyster mixture. Top each with bread crumbs and paprika and bake until the bread crumbs just begin to brown, 10 to 15 minutes.

# Carpetbagger Steak with Tasso Hollandaise

## CHEF JACQUES LEONARDI, JACQUES-IMO'S

*Jacques-Imo's, in Uptown New Orleans, produces a variety of local specialties crafted with a creative twist. This carpetbagger steak is a rich and spicy combination of compatible flavors. Make the hollandaise sauce first, and keep it warm in a double boiler over very low simmering water.*

### OYSTER TASSO HOLLANDAISE

10 shucked fresh oysters

the juices (liquor) from the oysters

1 pound (4 sticks) unsalted butter

1/4 pound (1 stick) margarine

yolks from 5 large eggs

1 tablespoon dry white wine

2 teaspoons fresh lemon juice

1 teaspoon Louisiana hot sauce

1/2 teaspoon worcestershire sauce

1 tablespoon olive oil

4 tablespoons ground or finely minced tasso ham

### CARPETBAGGER STEAK

12 shucked fresh oysters

the juices (liquor) from the oysters

2 teaspoons salt

2 teaspoons freshly ground black pepper

8 tablespoons (1 stick) butter

6 beef filets, 8 ounces each

1 1/2 cups blue cheese

1 tablespoon olive oil

1 whole red Bermuda or white Vidalia onion

**YIELD: 6 servings**

Strain the oyster liquor into a container to remove grit and refrigerate or freeze for future use. Chop the oysters coarsely and set them aside.

Melt the butter and margarine in a saucepan over medium heat. Remove from heat when completely melted and set aside. Pour water into the bottom of a double boiler over medium-high heat. In a mixing bowl combine the egg yolks, white wine, lemon juice, Louisiana hot sauce and worcestershire sauce, whisking to mix thoroughly When the water in the double boiler begins to boil, reduce heat to low and pour the egg mixture into the top pot. Continue whisking the mixture until it thickens.

Remove the double boiler from heat and, in a very slow steady stream, add the melted butter and margarine, whisking constantly until all melted butter has been added. Avoid cooking the egg yolks, which will curdle the sauce.

Grind or mince the tasso. Pour the olive oil into a heavy skillet and sauté the tasso. When the tasso is heated throughout, add the chopped oysters and stir the mixture well. Gradually stir the tasso and oyster mixture into the hollandaise sauce to mix everything thoroughly. Keep the sauce warm in the double boiler until ready to top the steaks. Preheat the oven broiler.

In the same skillet used to sauté the tasso and oysters, melt 4 tablespoons (1/2 stick) of the butter over medium heat. Add the oysters and their liquor and cook over medium-low heat until the oysters' edges just begin to curl, about 5 minutes. Remove from heat and hold in the warm skillet.

Slice a pocket in the side of each steak at the middle, cutting about three quarters of the way through. Place two whole oysters in each pocket. Closing the pockets with toothpicks is optional. Sprinkle the filets with salt and pepper. Melt the remaining 4 tablespoons of butter in a heavy skillet. When the butter is hot, sauté the steaks to the desired doneness and set them aside on a broiler pan.

Cut the onion into four slices, each about 1/4 inch thick. Add the olive oil to a second skillet. When the oil is hot, sauté the onion slices. When the slices are almost translucent, use a spatula to place each one on top of one of the steaks. Then top each onion slice with 2 tablespoons of the blue cheese.

Place the steaks on the middle rack of the oven and broil until the cheese has melted. Remove the steaks from the oven and arrange them on serving plates. Finish by drizzling with the steaks with hollandaise sauce, or serve the sauce on the side.

# P&J's Oysters Joseph

## SAL SUNSERI, SR.

*This recipe continues to be the one most often served when the current generation of the widespread Sunseri family gets together for a feast. Their father, the late Sal Sunseri, Sr. was the powerhouse who moved P&J Oysters forward, making it what it is today. He created Oysters Joseph, which was always his favorite dish.*

1/2 gallon shucked oysters

strained oyster liquor

1 stick unsalted butter or margarine

8 toes garlic, minced

3 green onions, finely chopped

3 cups seasoned Italian breadcrumbs

3 lemons

1/2 cup extra virgin olive oil

1 cup fresh grated Romano cheese

**YIELD: 10 to 12 servings**

Preheat the oven to Broil.

Strain the oyster liquor to remove grit. Set aside.

Chop the garlic and green onions. Set green onions aside. In a large heavy bottomed skillet, melt butter or margarine over a medium heat. Sauté minced garlic until soft and translucent, about 2 to 3 minutes. Add oysters and strained liquor. Cook oysters with sautéed garlic for about 3-5 minutes until the oysters plump and edges begin to curl.

Using a 9"-13" Pyrex dish or similar sized casserole dish, spread 1 cup of breadcrumbs evenly on the bottom of the dish. Spoon a layer of oysters and sautéed garlic mixture with 1/3 of the uncooked green onions and drizzle 1/3 of the olive oil on top of the breadcrumbs.

Add the second 1 cup layer of breadcrumbs and sprinkle a 1/3 cup layer of Romano cheese over them. Drizzle the second 1/3 of the olive oil on top of breadcrumbs and cheese then add the zest of 1 lemon as well as the juice of 1 lemon. On top of the layer spoon the remaining oysters and sautéed garlic mixture and the remaining uncooked green onions. Add the last layer of breadcrumbs and sprinkle remaining Romano cheese.

Cut 1 lemon in 1/8 inch slices and place on top of the cheese, breadcrumbs and drizzle remaining 1/3 olive oil. Broil on the oven's middle rack until cheese is golden brown and the dish is heated through, 4 to 5 minutes. Watch carefully.

Squeeze the juice of the last lemon on top of the casserole before serving.

The amount of ingredients can be reduced incrementally to produce a smaller quantity.

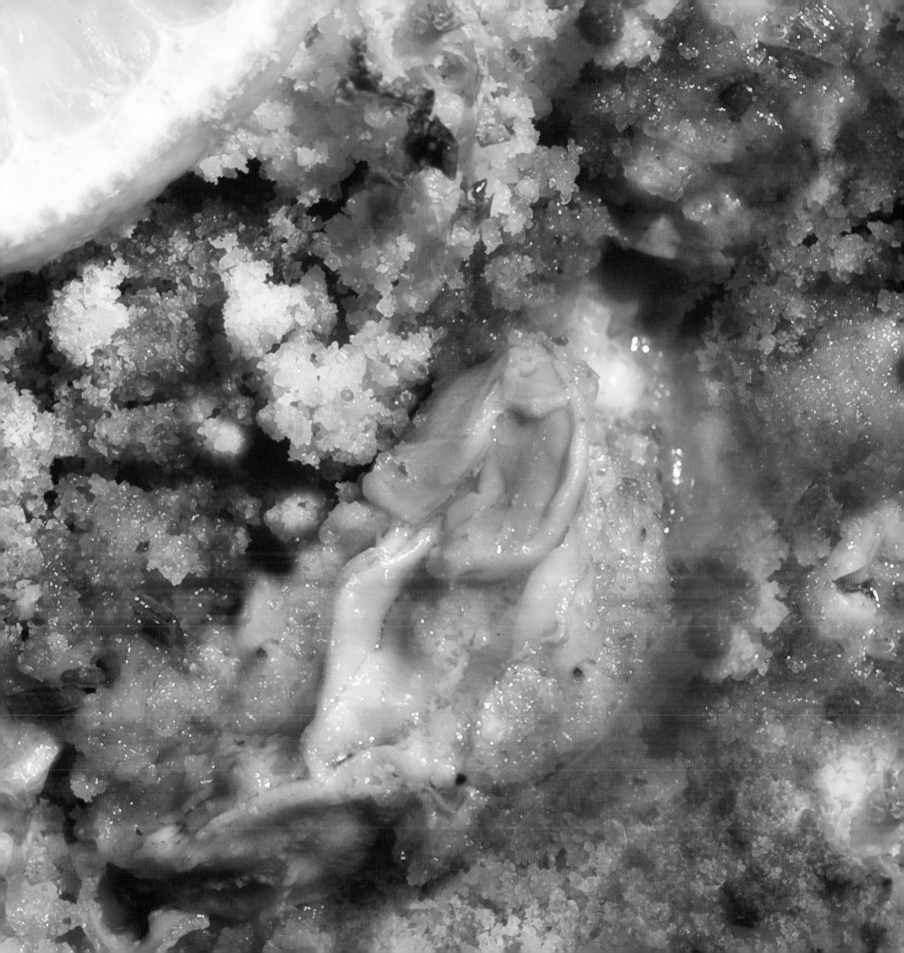

# Oysters Irene

## CHEF NICHOLAS SCALCO, IRENE'S CUISINE

*Always crowded, Irene's in the New Orleans French Quarter is simultaneously exciting and relaxed, a local's see-and-be-seen kind of place. Irene DiPietro's son, Nicholas Scalco, has assumed the reins in the kitchen, and is doing his mother proud, picking up on the Sicilian-American traditions that have always inspired the menus.*

12 shucked fresh oysters, bottom shells reserved

1 cup chopped pancetta or raw bacon

1 red sweet pepper, roasted, peeled, and finely chopped

1 cup grated Parmigiano-Reggiano cheese

3 tablespoons chopped flat-leaf (Italian) parsley

1 lemon, halved

**YIELD: 3 to 4 servings**

Strain the oyster juices (the "liquor") into a container to remove grit and refrigerate or freeze for future use. Scrub the oyster bottom shells clean under running water and set aside.

Preheat the oven broiler.

Prepare a half-shell tray large enough to hold the 12 oyster bottom shells, as described on page 14, using an oven-proof baking pan or a rimmed baking sheet. Set aside.

Place 1 oyster on each of the bottom shells and position each on the prepared half-shell tray. Top each oyster with a big pinch of pancetta, and broil until the pancetta is light brown and crispy.

Remove the tray from the oven and top each oyster with a pinch each of red pepper and cheese. Return the oysters to the oven broiler and broil until the cheese just begins to brown.

Arrange the oysters on a serving platter, sprinkle with a little parsley and lemon juice, and serve immediately.

# Baked Oysters with Brie Cream Sauce

## CHEF STEVE SCHWARZ, MAT & NADDIE'S

*Mat & Naddie's has adapted this recipe for the home oven and broiler. It actually results in something quite elegant. There are four parts to the recipe, three that require preparation prior to cooking the oysters. This must be done in advance, or even the day before. The oysters also may be cooked on a very hot grill, with the rack placed just above the white hot coals.*

### BAKING THE OYSTERS

24 shucked fresh oysters, with bottom shells reserved

4 cups rock salt

2 cups oyster marinade (below)

3 cups Brie cream sauce (next page)

1 cup shiitake "bacon" (next page)

1 tablespoon ground sweet paprika

3 tablespoons minced parsley

### YIELD: 4 to 6 servings

Preheat the oven to 500°F.

Strain the oyster juices (the "liquor") into a container to remove grit and refrigerate or freeze the liquor for future use. Set the oysters aside. Scrub the oyster bottom shells clean under running water.

Prepare a sufficient number of half-shell trays to hold 24 oyster bottom shells, as described on page 14, using a large rimmed baking sheet. Place the tray(s) on the top oven rack, about 5 inches from the heat source.

Soak the shucked oysters briefly in the oyster marinade. Warm the Brie cream sauce through, but do not bring it to a boil.

When the bottom shells are extremely hot, turn the oven to the broil function. Pull out the oven rack and spoon one oyster onto each bottom shell. Top each one proportionately with some of the Parmigiano-Reggiano and slide in the oven rack so the oysters are underneath the hot broiler. Cook until the cheese is bubbly, about 3 minutes. Remove the half-shell tray(s) from broiler and immediately spoon about 2 tablespoons of the Brie cream sauce on top of each oyster. Garnish each one with a strip or two of shiitake bacon and a pinch each of paprika and parsley. Place 1 cup of hot rock salt on each of four plates. Place 6 oysters onto each bed of salt and serve immediately.

### OYSTER MARINADE

1/3 cup fresh lemon juice

1 1/2 teaspoons worcestershire sauce

3 tablespoons Louisiana-style hot sauce

3 cloves garlic, smashed and very finely chopped

1/2 teaspoon salt

1/2 teaspoon freshly ground black pepper

1 cup vegetable oil

3 tablespoons unsalted butter, melted

### YIELD: 2 cups

In a large bowl, combine all ingredients except the vegetable oil and butter. Whisk in the oil and butter. Set aside. (The marinade may be kept for up to one week in the refrigerator.)

*(see recipes for Brie Cream Sauce and Shiitake "Bacon" on next page)*

*(recipes continued from previous page)*

## BRIE CREAM SAUCE

2 tablespoons vegetable oil or unsalted butter

1/2 medium onion, roughly chopped

2 cloves garlic, smashed and chopped

leaves from 1 rosemary sprig, chopped

leaves from 1 thyme sprig, chopped

1 whole bay leaf

1 1/2 cups dry white wine

2 cups heavy cream

6 ounces Brie cheese, cut into chunks

**YIELD: About 3 cups**

In a saucepan, warm the oil over medium-low heat. Add the onion, garlic, rosemary, thyme and bay leaf and sauté until softened. Add the wine, bring to a simmer, and reduce by about half. Stir in the cream and simmer again until the liquid is reduced by about half. Remove from the heat and whisk in the Brie. Let the mixture stand until the cheese melts, then retrieve and discard the bay leaf. In a blender or food processor, puree the mixture until smooth, then pass through a fine strainer. (This sauce may be kept, covered, in the refrigerator for several days.)

## SHIITAKE "BACON"

12 shiitake mushrooms, brushed clean

1 quart canola oil

**YIELD: About 1 cup**

Remove the mushroom stems and reserve for other use. Slice the caps into thick julienne strips.

In a large, heavy pot no more than one third filled with oil, or a deep fryer, heat the oil to 300°F.

Lower the mushroom strips into the hot oil and fry until all the sizzling stops. Lay the fried strips on a rack to cool and dry. When the strips are cool, they should be very dry. (The "bacon" may be stored in a cool and dry place for up to two days.)

# Oyster Biscuit Pudding

## CHEF CHRIS LUSK, CAFÉ ADELAIDE

*Their beloved aunt, the late Adelaide Brennan is the namesake and inspiration for Ti Adelaide Martin and Lally Brennan's kicky restaurant. Chef Chris Lusk cooks in a lavish and theatrical manner appropriate to Adelaide's memory.*

15 P & J Oysters

2 teaspoons unsalted butter

1 medium white onion, diced

1 stalk celery, diced

2 cloves garlic, minced

1 bell pepper, diced

1/2 cup Pernod or Herbsaint

1 quart heavy cream

4 eggs

1 teaspoon fresh parsley chopped

1 teaspoon fresh thyme chopped

1 teaspoon fresh oregano chopped

8 buttermilk biscuits* crumbled

1 teaspoon Louisiana-style hot sauce

Salt and pepper to taste

1/2 cup grated Parmigiano-Reggiano

**YIELD: 8 servings**

Preheat oven to 350°F.

In a large, heavy-bottomed skillet, melt the butter over medium heat. Sauté onion, celery, garlic and bell pepper in the butter until onion is translucent. Deglaze pan by swirling the contents with the Pernod or Herbsaint. Add heavy cream to the pan, mix contents thoroughly together and cook on medium heat for 5 minutes. Set aside and allow the mixture to cool. In a large bowl combine lightly beaten eggs, herbs, biscuits, hot sauce and cooled cream mixture.

Rough chop oysters and combine with biscuit mixture. Season with salt and pepper to taste then divide mixture in 8 heatproof ramekins. Top with cheese and bake at 350°F for 8 to10 minutes or until mixture sets. A straw or toothpick inserted into the mixture should come out clean.

*Use prepared biscuits or your favorite recipe.

# Soups,
# Gumbos
# and Stews

*Some of the most delicious oyster meals consist of soups, gumbos or stews. The versatile oyster can take these recipes from the very simple to the sublime.*

*A system of ropes and pulleys, nets, buckets and conveyer belts bring the oysters from the beds to be washed and iced, ready for delivery.*

# Mom's Oyster Gumbo

**BOBBIE SUNSERI**

*Oysters are one of the most popular foods in New Orleans, with recipes to match. The Sunseri family considers this gumbo one of their savory holiday favorites. Who would know more about oysters than the Sunseri family?*

72 (8 dozen) shucked fresh oysters

the juices (liquor) from the oysters

1 cup vegetable oil or bacon fat

1 1/2 cups flour

3 large yellow onions, medium dice

1 green sweet pepper, medium dice

1 1/2 cups thin-sliced celery

2 quarts chicken stock, unsalted and preferably fresh (page 210)

salt and freshly ground black pepper, to taste

2 whole bay leaves

1/2 cup chopped parsley

1 tablespoon filé powder

Louisiana-style hot sauce, to taste

cooked rice

1 cup chopped green onions or chives, for garnish

**YIELD: 1 1/2 gallons**

Strain the oyster liquor into a bowl to remove grit. Set both the liquor and the oysters aside.

In heavy, 8-quart Dutch oven heat the oil or bacon fat over medium heat. Add the flour and blend the two thoroughly. Reduce heat to low-to-moderate and prepare a light-dark roux, by stirring and scraping the mixture constantly until it is the color of peanut butter. This should take between 30 and 45 minutes. During the process, the heat level will need to be adjusted to prevent the flour from scorching.

Add the onion, celery, and green sweet pepper to the roux and cook another 15 minutes, stirring constantly, until the vegetables are soft.

In a saucepan, warm 2 quarts of the chicken stock and gradually add it, cup by cup, to the roux and vegetables in the pot, stirring constantly until the roux is incorporated into the stock. Simmer, stirring often, until the vegetables almost liquefy, about 1 hour.

Add the oysters and the oyster juices to the stock, along with the salt, pepper and bay leaves, then reduce the heat and simmer 15 minutes.

Remove from heat and sprinkle with parsley and filé powder. Add salt, pepper and hot sauce to taste. Allow the gumbo to rest for 15 minutes before stirring or serving.

At serving time, if the gumbo has cooled more than desired, return it to the stove and bring it back up to a simmer. Serve over cooked rice. Garnish with chopped green onions or chives.

# Mom's Fried-Oyster Gumbo

**BOBBIE SUNSERI**

*This is an excellent way to enjoy fried oysters in a hearty gumbo, and at the same time, make use of frozen oyster liquor.*

### GUMBO

1 1/2 cups vegetable oil
2 cups all-purpose flour
2 large yellow onions, chopped
4 celery stalks, chopped
3 green sweet peppers, chopped
4 quarts of one or more of the following:
salt-free fish stock, fresh or canned
oyster liquor
clam juice
1 sprig fresh rosemary
1 teaspoon dried thyme
1/4 teaspoon cayenne pepper
cooked white rice
4 slices bacon, fried and crumbled,
for garnish, optional

### FRIED OYSTERS

24 to 32 shucked fresh oysters
1 pound self-rising flour
1 pound self-rising corn meal
1 teaspoon salt
freshly ground black pepper, to taste
2 quarts peanut oil

**YIELD: 6 to 8 servings**

In a 6-quart Dutch oven or heavy pot, make the roux. Completing the roux will take anywhere from 30 to 45 minutes. Cooking slowly on low heat is the secret to a successful roux. Be careful not to let the flour scorch. Heat the oil over medium heat, very gradually adding the flour while cooking and stirring constantly, until the roux reaches the color of dark-mahogany brown. Add the chopped onions, peppers and celery. (This will temporarily stop the cooking process.)

Cook the roux until the vegetables are tender and becoming translucent, continuing to stir constantly. As the vegetables cook, their sugar will be released and the roux will darken even more as the liquid evaporates.

In a separate 6-quart stock pot, warm the stock. Then add it, cup by cup, to the roux and vegetables in the other pot, stirring constantly Next add the rosemary, thyme and cayenne pepper. Simmer, covered, for 1 hour. Taste the gumbo for seasoning and add salt and pepper to taste. While it is simmering, prepare the fried oysters. If the gumbo has cooled down, continue warming it until all the oysters have been fried and are hot.

Strain the oyster juices (the "liquor") into a container to remove grit and refrigerate or freeze for future use. Set the oysters themselves aside.

Using a large roasting pan 2 to 3 inches deep, combine the flour, corn meal, salt and pepper. Coat each oyster by tossing it in the flour-and-corn-meal mixture. Coat each oyster completely. Do not shake off the excess coating. Repeat the procedure with all of the oysters.

If not using an electric fryer, place a large, heavy pot or Dutch oven no more than 1/3 full of oil over high heat (or, set a deep fryer to 350°F). Set the oven temperature to 200°F. Line a baking sheet with paper towels and place it in the oven. When the oil reaches the correct temperature, dredge the oysters, a few at a time, in the flour-and-corn-meal mixture, shaking off the excess. Using tongs, drop each oyster in the hot oil and fry until golden, 3 to 5 minutes. Using a slotted spoon, transfer the oysters to the baking sheet in the warm oven until all of them have been fried.

To serve the gumbo, add cooked white rice to six to eight large, shallow soup bowls. Ladle the gumbo into the bowls. Float four to six fried oysters on top of each bowl of gumbo. Garnish with crumbled fried bacon if desired. Serve with hot French bread.

# P&J's Oysters Rockefeller Bisque

## AL SUNSERI

*Al Sunseri won the Times-Picayune's famous annual recipe contest with this salute to P&J Oysters. Since this magnificent soup is very rich, it may also be served in demitasse cups, doubling the number of servings.*

1/2 gallon plus 1 quart shucked fresh oysters

1/2 cup (1 stick) melted unsalted butter

5 green onions, chopped

1/4 head iceberg lettuce, chopped

6 cloves minced garlic

5 stalks finely chopped celery

4 (10-ounce) packages thawed frozen spinach, squeezed dry and chopped

1/4 teaspoon cayenne pepper

2 tablespoons Chef Paul's Seafood Magic

1/2 gallon whole milk

1 quart half and half

zest of 1 lemon

juice of 2 lemons

1 cup freshly grated Romano cheese

1/2 cup Herbsaint or Pernod anisette liqueur

salt to taste

**YIELD: 30 servings**

Strain the oysters liquor to remove grit. Set liquor aside and freeze for future use.

Chop celery, lettuce, spinach, green onions, and garlic. Set aside 1/2 cup of green onions for garnish. In a large, heavy Dutch oven or cast-iron pot, melt the butter over low heat. Add the spinach, celery, lettuce, garlic, green onion, cayenne and Chef Paul's Seafood Magic and sauté until the vegetables are soft, about 10 to 15 minutes, stirring occasionally. Add 1 pint of the oysters (about 24 oysters) to the sautéed ingredients and cook for an additional 5 minutes.

Add the milk and half and half. Pour the mixture in batches into a blender, filling it halfway and blend throughly. In a 2 gallon stockpot, place each batch as it is blended. (Only fill blender 1/2 way when blending.) When all of the mixture has been blended, stir the anisette liqueur, cheese, lemon zest, juice of two lemons, and remaining milk into the stockpot. Add all of the remaining oysters and heat over a low flame, stirring occasionally until the oysters are plump and their edges just begin to curl. Add salt to taste.

For a thinner soup, stir in more milk until the desired consistency is achieved. Garnish with green onions. Ladle into bowls or cups and serve. The amount of ingredients can be reduced incrementally to produce less bisque.

# Oysters Stewed in Cream

## ARCHIE A. CASBARIAN, ARNAUD'S RESTAURANT

*Arnaud's late proprietor Archie A. Casbarian placed Oysters Stewed in Cream on his first menu when he restored the historic French Quarter restaurant. His family continues to maintain his high standards, and can be coaxed to bring out this fine oyster stew on special occasions. Jane, his wife, his son Archie and his daughter Katy are the proprietors.*

3 1/2 cups water

24 shucked fresh oysters

the juices (liquor) from the oysters

1 tablespoon plus 1/4 cup unsalted butter

1/2 cup chopped yellow onion

1/2 cup chopped celery

1/2 cup chopped green onions

1/2 teaspoon minced garlic

1/8 teaspoon dried thyme

1/8 teaspoon ground red pepper

1 bay leaf

3/4 cup heavy cream

2 cups whole milk

1/2 cup all-purpose flour

1 teaspoon salt

1/4 teaspoon freshly ground white peppercorns

**YIELD: 4 to 6 servings**

Strain the oyster liquor to remove grit and set aside.

In a medium-size saucepan bring the water to a boil. Add the oysters and the oyster liquor, and continue to simmer for 3 minutes, until the edges just begin to curl.

Remove the oysters with a slotted spoon. Increase the heat to medium-high to reduce the amount of water and oyster liquor to 2 1/2 cups. Reserve this liquid.

In a Dutch oven over medium heat, melt 1 tablespoon of the butter. When it is hot, add the celery, yellow onion and green onion. Cook, stirring constantly until the vegetables are soft. Stir in the 2 1/2 cups of reserved liquid and the garlic, thyme, red pepper and bay leaf. Bring to a boil, then stir in the cream. Reduce the heat and simmer for 5 minutes. Stir in the milk and return to a simmer. Set aside.

Melt the remaining 1/4 cup butter in a small saucepan over low heat. Add the flour, stirring with a wire whisk until smooth. Cook 4 minutes, stirring constantly, or until smooth. (The mixture will be very thick.)

Gradually add the flour mixture to the milk mixture, stirring until they are blended. Add the oysters, salt and white pepper. Heat the stewed oysters thoroughly. Remove from heat, discard the bay leaf and serve immediately.

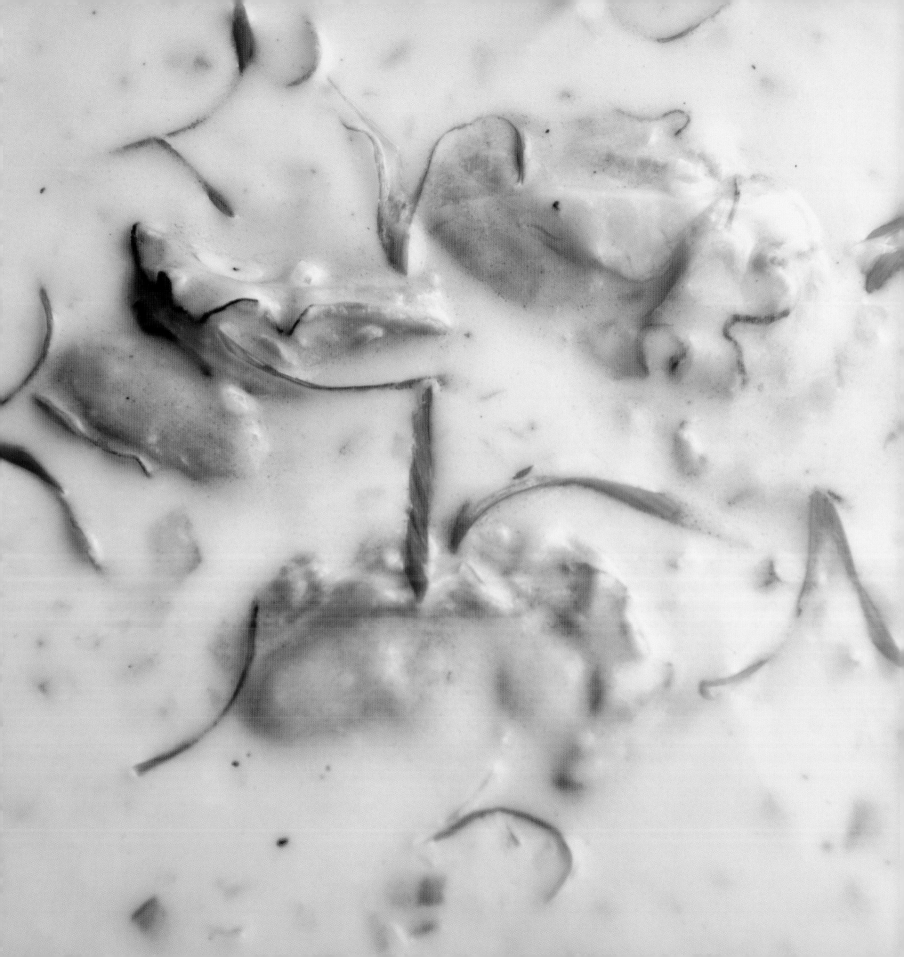

# Oyster and Artichoke Soup

## CHEF TOMMY MANDINA, MANDINA'S

*One of the city's iconic establishments, Mandina's has been serving generations of New Orleanians authentic Creole-Italian specialties at its Mid-City location. The family has occupied the old Canal Street building since 1898, first as a grocery store, then into another of the city's many family-owned and operated eateries.*

1 1/2 quarts water

1 1/2 quarts chicken stock, homemade (page 210), or prepared

1 bay leaf

1 teaspoon dried oregano

2 tablespoons granulated garlic

4 ounces vegetable oil

8 tablespoons flour

1/2 cup green onions, trimmed and coarsely chopped

2 celery stalks, finely chopped

1 yellow onion, finely chopped

2 (14-ounce) cans artichoke hearts, drained and chopped

2 tablespoons fresh parsley, finely chopped

Kosher or sea salt and cayenne pepper to taste

48 fresh shucked oysters, coarsely chopped

the juices (liquor) from the oysters

Louisiana hot sauce to taste

freshly ground black pepper to taste

thyme sprigs for garnish

French or Italian bread, for serving

**YIELD: 8 2 cup servings or 16 1 cup servings**

Strain the oyster liquor to remove grit and set aside. Cover and refrigerate the oysters while preparing the soup. Chop while the soup is simmering.

In a 1 to 2 gallon heavy bottomed stockpot or Dutch oven add the water and bring to a boil. Add the chicken stock bay leaf, oregano, and garlic.

Using a heavy bottomed medium sized skillet, make a blonde roux by warming the oil over a medium low heat and gradually whisking in the flour, stirring continuously until it is a light tan. This will take 10 to 15 minutes. Gradually stir the roux into the stockpot of liquids and seasonings.

Add the celery, green onions, parsley and onions to the mixture and bring to a boil for 15 minutes. Add the oysters and strained oyster liquor to the mixture. Add the chopped artichoke hearts to the soup. Return the mixture to a boil.

Remove the bay leaf and discard.

Adjust seasonings with Louisiana hot sauce, salt and pepper to taste.

Ladle the soup into bowls, garnish with thyme sprigs and serve with crusty French or Italian bread.

# Oyster Soup

## CJ GERDES, CASAMENTO'S

*Walls clad in glistening, blue and white ceramic tiles are the sparkling backdrop for Casamento's oysters, more oysters and other seafood in a variety of guises. The old-fashioned restaurant in Uptown New Orleans maintains an ages-old operating schedule, closing from early to late summer.*

24 shucked fresh oysters

the juices (liquor) from the oysters

1/2 cup finely chopped celery

1/2 cup finely chopped green onion

1/2 cup finely chopped yellow onion

4 tablespoons (1/2 stick) unsalted butter

1/2 teaspoon minced garlic

1/8 teaspoon dried thyme

1/8 teaspoon ground red pepper

1 whole bay leaf

3/4 cup heavy whipping cream

2 cups whole milk

1/2 cup all-purpose flour

1 teaspoon salt

1/4 teaspoon freshly ground white pepper

**YIELD: 4 to 6 servings**

Drain the oysters in a sieve over a large measuring cup. Add enough water to the oyster liquor to make 2 1/2 cups of liquid.

In a medium saucepan over high heat bring the oyster liquor and water to boil. Reduce heat to medium-low, add the oysters and cook for 3 minutes. Remove the oysters with a slotted spoon and set them and the liquid aside.

In a large, heavy pot or Dutch oven, over medium heat, cook the celery, green onion and yellow onion in 1 tablespoon of the butter, stirring constantly until the vegetables are soft.

Stir in the 2 1/2 cups of reduced liquid, along with the garlic, thyme, red pepper and bay leaf. Bring to a boil. Stir in the cream, reduce the heat and simmer for 5 minutes. Stir in the milk and return to a simmer.

In a separate, small saucepan, melt the remaining 3 tablespoons of butter over low heat. Add the flour, and stir continuously until the mixture is smooth. Cook for 1 minute, still over low heat, stirring constantly, then cook for about 3 more minutes. (The mixture should be very thick.)

Remove the flour-and-butter mixture from heat and gradually add it to the other saucepan containing the cream, milk and seasonings. Stir with a wire whisk until everything is blended.

Add the oysters, salt and white pepper and stir well. Cook until thoroughly heated. Remove from the heat, discard the bay leaf and serve immediately.

# Oyster Stew

## TRACY LANDRY, DON'S SEAFOOD HUT

*The New Orleans area abounds with numerous family-owned and operated restaurants. Don's, in the suburb of Metairie, is one of them that take pride in their heritage and togetherness.*

3 tablespoons unsalted butter

2 tablespoons chopped green onion

1/4 white onion, minced

1 stalk celery, minced

3 tablespoons all-purpose flour

4 cups whole milk

24 shucked fresh oysters

the juices (liquor) from the oysters

salt and freshly ground black pepper, to taste

2 tablespoons minced parsley

1/8 teaspoon ground paprika

**YIELD: 2 servings**

Melt the butter in a sauté pan over medium-high heat. Add and sauté the green onion, white onion and celery until softened. Stir in the flour and stir constantly until smooth. Stir in the milk and bring to a simmer, stirring constantly.

Add the oysters and oyster liquor and simmer for about 2 minutes more, until the edges of the oysters just begin to curl. Remove from heat and season to taste with salt and pepper. Scatter with the parsley and top with a dash of paprika. Serve immediately.

# Oyster Stew with Caramelized Onions and Parmesan Toast
## CHEFS JIM CONTE AND MATTHEW GUIDRY, MEAUXBAR BISTRO

*This was inspired by the oyster pan roast served at the Oyster Bar at New York's Grand Central Station. It's an absolute favorite at Meauxbar Bistro in New Orleans during the short, chilly winter months when Louisiana oysters are at their best.*

### CRÈME FRAÎCHE

1 cup heavy cream

1 tablespoon buttermilk

**YIELD: 6 servings**

Heat the heavy cream to 95°F and combine it with the buttermilk in a container with a tilted lid to create a narrow gap. Let the mixture sit at room temperature for 24 hours before refrigerating, then refrigerate until chilled, about 1 hour.

### PARMESAN TOAST

2 garlic cloves, minced

1/2 cup olive oil

1/2 cup grated Parmigiano-Reggiano cheese

6 French rolls cut lengthwise into 4 slices

Preheat the oven to 500°F.

Smash the garlic with the side of a knife and mince well. Combine the garlic and olive oil in a small mixing bowl. Brush the garlic and oil onto each cut side of bread and sprinkle generously with grated Parmigiano-Reggiano. Toast the slices in the oven for 5 minutes or until they are golden.

### STEW

66 shucked fresh oysters

4 cups juices from the oysters or clam juice

3 tablespoons olive oil

1 1/2 tablespoons unsalted butter

2 Spanish onions, thinly sliced

1 1/2 tablespoon sugar

4 garlic cloves, minced

3 Yukon Gold potatoes, skin on, cut into 1/2-inch dice

salt and freshly ground black pepper, to taste

1 1/2 cups heavy cream

1/3 cup crème fraîche

2 tablespoons finely chopped fresh tarragon

If using the juices from the oysters (the "liquor") strain the liquor into a quart-size (or larger) measuring container to remove grit and produce 4 cups. Set the oysters and their liquor aside.

Heat the olive oil and butter in saucepan over medium heat. Add the onions and sugar and cook until the onions are caramelized.

Add the garlic and cook for 2 minutes. Add the oyster or clam juices to the onions and bring the liquid to a boil. Add the potatoes and cook 5 minutes. Add heavy cream and bring to simmer. Whisk in the crème fraîche. Add salt and pepper to taste. Add the oysters and tarragon and cook until the edges of the oysters just begin to curl, about 5 minutes. Serve hot with warm parmesan toast.

# P&J's Oyster and Brie Soup

*Not only are oysters grilled with Brie divine, the two are also grand partners when served in a velvety soup. This recipe was created by Al Sunseri following a Thanksgiving dinner when there were a few leftovers. The soup is so rich it may be served as half portions in demitasses.*

36 shucked fresh oysters (2 pints)

1/2 cup (1 sticks) unsalted butter

1/2 cup all-purpose flour

1 pint heavy cream

1 1/2 teaspoons cayenne pepper

8-12 ounces Brie cheese, rind removed and cheese diced

1 cup finely chopped green onions (white and light-green parts)

salt and pepper to taste

crusty French bread, for serving

**YIELD: 8 teacups or 16 demitasses**

Strain oysters to remove liquor and grit. Set liquor aside and freeze for future use.

Chop green onions and set aside 1/4 cup for garnish.

In a one gallon pot, melt the butter over a medium heat and sauté garlic and green onions until translucent. Add the drained oysters and simmer until the oysters curl, 2 to 3 minutes. Stir in heavy cream, half and half, and cheese, continue stirring until cheese melts. Add salt and pepper to taste, cover and let stand for 10 minutes. Ladle into bowls or cups and garnish with green remaining green onions and serve, with crusty French bread on the side.

# Old-Fashioned Oyster Chowder

*A steaming bowl of this chowder, based on a traditional recipe, should always be accompanied by a loaf of French bread or, if you must, oyster crackers.*

4 ounces (1 stick) unsalted butter

1/2 cup finely chopped celery

1/2 cup finely chopped yellow onion

1/2 cup finely chopped carrots

1 large potato, peeled and diced 1/2 inch

2 1/2 cups fish stock or bottled clam juice

2 1/ 2 cups chicken broth

2 cups light cream

juice of half a lemon

12 shucked fresh oysters

the juices (liquor) from the oysters

salt and freshly ground black pepper, to taste

chopped parsley, for garnish

crusty French bread, for serving

**YIELD: 4 to 6 servings**

Strain the oyster liquor to remove grit and set aside.

In a large saucepan, warm the butter over medium-low heat until melted. Add and sauté the celery and onion in the butter until the vegetables are tender.

Add the potato, carrots, fish stock, chicken broth, cream and lemon juice. Bring to a very low simmer and cook, stirring frequently, until the chowder starts to thicken, about 25 minutes.

Meanwhile, coarsely chop six of the oysters. When the soup has thickened, add the chopped oysters and oyster liquor, and bring back to a simmer. Add the remaining 6 whole oysters to the pan and return, once again, to a simmer. Stir in salt and pepper to taste.

Sprinkle with chopped parsley and serve hot, with crusty French bread on the side.

# Casseroles, Pastas and Pies

*Succulent oysters blend with pastry, bread crumbs, vegetables and other ingredients to create a fascinating, almost endless array of recipes suited for uptown, downtown and back of town.*

*The rake and net assembly is lowered and scoops along the bottom of the oyster bed then is drawn back into the boat. The fisherman sizes and washes the oysters before they are iced down in burlap sacks. The small oysters are returned to their bed for another day.*

# P&J's Louisiana Oyster Pie

*Individual small pies or a single family-size one are equally lovely to look at and delicious to eat. This recipe does not call for a traditional pie crust, but instead makes use of phyllo dough or puff pastry as a flaky topping.*

12 shucked fresh oysters

the juices (liquor) from the oysters

5 slices raw bacon

1 tablespoon butter

8 ounces sliced mushrooms

1 small yellow onion, chopped

1/2 cup chopped green onion

2 cloves garlic, minced

1/4 cup flour

salt and freshly ground black pepper, to taste

dash cayenne pepper

1/4 cup chopped parsley

2 tablespoon fresh lemon juice

8 ounces frozen phyllo sheets or puff pastry

**YIELD: 4 to 6 servings**

Strain the oyster juices (the "liquor") into a container to remove grit and refrigerate or freeze for future use.

Preheat the oven to 400°F.

In a skillet, cook the bacon until crisp. Remove the cooked slices with a slotted spoon and drain on absorbent paper. Crumble the bacon.

Grease a 9-inch pie plate with the butter.

In the skillet, sauté the mushrooms, yellow onion and green onions in the bacon fat for about 5 minutes, or until tender. Add the garlic and cook for 1 minute more. Whisk in the flour, salt, black pepper and cayenne. Stir in the oysters, crumbled bacon, parsley and lemon juice.

Turn the oyster mixture into the pie plate and top with the phyllo or puff pastry. Make several slits in the top to allow for heat to escape. Bake for 15 to 20 minutes, or until the crust is golden brown.

# P&J's Oyster Triangles

*As avid oyster fans, members of the Sunseri family enjoy pleasing guests with tasty canapés. This recipe is simple to prepare, easy to serve and, obviously, a treat to look forward to at Sunseri family gatherings.*

12 shucked fresh oysters

the juices (liquor) from the oysters

4 tablespoons (1/2 stick) butter

2 tablespoons all-purpose flour

5 green onions, chopped

2 tablespoons minced garlic

1/4 cup finely chopped mushroom caps

6 artichoke hearts, either frozen or canned, finely chopped

1/4 cup finely chopped fresh spinach

3 tablespoons chicken broth, fresh or canned

1 sheet frozen puff pastry, 9-by-9 inches, thawed

1 or 2 dashes Creole seasoning ( page 219)

3 or 4 dashes Louisiana hot sauce

**YIELD: 9 appetizers (3-inch triangles) or 18 canapes (1-1/2-inch triangles)**

Strain the oyster juices (the "liquor") into a large measuring cup to remove grit. Reserve 1/4 cup.

Cut the oysters into quarters.

Begin by making the filling for the triangles. In a saucepan, prepare a blond roux by cooking 2 tablespoons (1/4 stick) of the butter and all of the flour together for 5 minutes on medium-low heat, stirring continuously to ensure even cooking. Cook until the roux is golden or light caramel in color. Add the green onions and garlic and cook, stirring occasionally, until the onions and garlic are soft.

Add the mushrooms and the remaining 2 tablespoons of butter to the saucepan. When the butter melts, add the artichoke hearts and cook them with the mushrooms for 2 to 3 minutes. Stir in the spinach and chicken broth. Cook for about 3 minutes. Stir in the Creole seasoning mix, Louisiana hot sauce to taste, the quartered oysters and reserved oyster liquor. Cook for about 3 minutes more, stirring constantly. Remove from heat and cool to room temperature before assembling the triangles.

Preheat the oven to 400°F.

With a long, sharp knife, cut the square sheet of pastry horizontally into thirds, then cut vertically twice to yield nine 3-inch squares. Place a spoonful of the filling mixture into the center of each square of pastry. Fold over the pastry to form triangles that will measure 3 inches on the long side. (For smaller canapés, cut the triangle in half from the point to the long side.) Crimp the edges of the triangles together with the tines of a fork and place the filled triangles on a greased baking sheet. Bake for 15 to 20 minutes, or until golden brown. Cool for 4 to 5 minutes and serve.

# Oyster Patties

## THE DEGRUSHA FAMILY, JOHNNY'S PO-BOYS

*Johnny's, in the New Orleans French Quarter, is famous for more than producing sterling versions of the city's favorite sandwich. These tasty morsels, when placed in small, medium or large phyllo pastry shells, can be used as canapé, appetizers or entrées.*

36 shucked fresh oysters

the juices (liquor) from the oysters

8 tablespoons (1 stick) salted butter

1 medium yellow onion, finely chopped

1/4 cup parsley, finely chopped

3 green onions, finely chopped

1 celery stalk, finely chopped

4 garlic cloves, finely chopped

2 tablespoons all-purpose flour

6 ounces half-and-half

salt and freshly ground black pepper, to taste

Louisiana hot sauce, to taste, optional

72 small, 12 medium or 6 large frozen phyllo-pastry shells

**YIELD: 72 canapés, 12 appetizers or 6 main-course servings**

Preheat oven to 325°F.

Strain the oyster liquor to remove grit and set aside. Chop the oysters coarsely and set aside.

In a medium-size saucepan over low heat, slowly melt the butter. When it is hot, add the yellow onion, parsley, green onions, celery and garlic. Cook, stirring occasionally, until the vegetables are tender. Add the flour and stir until it is fully incorporated into the mixture. Add the half-and-half and stir to mix thoroughly. Add the chopped oysters and continue cooking for about 5 minutes. Add salt and pepper to taste. If using the Louisiana hot sauce, add it to taste also.

For a thicker filling, add an additional tablespoon of flour and continue cooking for 3 or 4 minutes to remove the raw flour taste. Or for a thinner filling, add more half-and-half.

Fill the phyllo-pastry shells and bake 10 to 15 minutes, according to the size and number of the pastry shells, until the sauce is bubbly.

# P&J's Oyster Puffs

*These bite-size hors d'oeuvres can be served with either a peppery cocktail sauce (page 217) or a beurre blanc (page 215) for dipping.*

1/2 cup shucked fresh oysters

1 cup water

1/2 cup butter

1 cup all-purpose flour

1/4 teaspoon salt

4 large eggs

**YIELD: 20 puffs**

Drain the juices (the "liquor") from the oysters with a strainer to remove grit, collecting the juices in a container and refrigerate or freeze them for future use.

Chop the oysters coarsely and set aside.

Preheat the oven to 400°F.

Combine the water and butter in a saucepan over high heat. When the water reaches a rolling boil, reduce the heat to low and stir in the flour and salt, stirring vigorously until the mixture forms a ball, about 1 minute. Add the eggs one at a time to the dough, beating with a fork until the mixture is smooth. Be careful not to cook the eggs. Stir in the chopped oysters.

To form the puffs, drop 1 slightly rounded measuring teaspoonful of the dough onto an un-greased cookie sheet, and repeat until 20 balls of dough are arranged on the sheet. Bake until the dough is puffed and golden brown, about 15 to 25 minutes. Serve hot with warm beurre blanc or chilled cocktail sauce for dipping.

# Oyster and Mushroom Tart

## CHEF TENNEY FLYNN, GARY WOLLERMAN, GW FINS

*GW Fins serves seafood flown in from around the world, but they rely on P&J Oysters for some of their most delectable recipes. This recipe calls for demi-glace, which also can be purchased at specialty markets, on the Internet or by mail order. A substitute can be made by reducing one 15-ounce can of concentrated beef consommé to 1/4 cup over high heat.*

### THE MUSHROOMS

1 ounce dried porcini mushrooms

1/4 cup extra-virgin olive oil

8 tablespoons (1 stick) unsalted butter

2 tablespoons finely chopped French shallot

1/2 pound shiitake mushrooms

1 pound oyster mushrooms

2 tablespoons dry white wine

2 tablespoons brandy

salt and freshly ground black pepper, to taste

2 teaspoons minced parsley

1/2 teaspoon minced fresh chervil

1/4 teaspoon finely snipped chives

**YIELD: 8 individual tarts**

Scrub the mushrooms under running water without mixing the three varieties. Cut the shiitake and oyster mushrooms in thick slices and set them aside, along with the whole porcini mushrooms.

Place the whole porcinis in a heat-proof bowl with 1/2 cup very hot water and turn them to coat them with the water. Let the porcinis stand for 20 minutes to absorb the water, tossing them again once or twice. Squeeze them over the bowl to remove as much water as possible, reserving the soaking liquid. Chop the mushrooms coarsely and set them aside.

Place the oil and butter in a large sauté pan over medium heat, and heat them until the butter melts. Add the chopped shallots and cook until soft. Raise the heat level to high and add the sliced shiitake mushrooms. Sauté the shiitakes for 2 minutes. Add the chopped porcinis and the sliced oyster mushrooms and cook for 2 to 3 minutes more, stirring continuously. Add the white wine and the reserved mushroom-soaking water, and continue cooking, uncovered, until the mixture is barely moist. Finally, add the brandy, salt, pepper, parsley chervil and chives. Reduce the heat to very low and let the flavors infuse for about 5 minutes more. Set the sautéed mushrooms aside.

### THE ROUX

1 tablespoon vegetable oil

1 tablespoon all-purpose flour

In a small sauté pan over medium heat, add the oil and whisk in the flour. Stir constantly until a dark peanut brown color has developed. It will require about 30 minutes.

*(recipes for Sauce and Final Assembly on next page)*

### THE SAUCE

40 shucked fresh oysters

2 cups oyster juices (liquor)

2 tablespoons butter

1 tablespoon finely chopped French shallots

1/4 cup dry white wine

2 tablespoons dark roux

2 ounces (1/4 cup) demi-glace (page 213)

salt and freshly ground black pepper, to taste

2 teaspoons finely chopped parsley

1 teaspoon finely chopped fresh chervil

12 teaspoon finely snipped fresh chives

Drain the oysters in a strainer over a large bowl to collect the liquor. Measure 2 cups of the oyster liquor and set them aside. Reserve the oysters themselves for the final stage of the recipe preparation.

Place the butter in a medium sauté pan over high heat. When it is melted, add the shallots and cook for 2 to 3 minutes, or until just soft. Add the wine and deglaze the pan. Then add the oyster liquor and bring the liquid to a simmer.

Whisk in the dark roux, and, continuing to whisk constantly, simmer the mixture until it reduces by 1/4 and is thick enough to coat a spoon. Stir in the demi-glace, salt, pepper, parsley, chervil and chives. Remove from heat and set aside.

### FINAL ASSEMBLY

2 tablespoons unsalted butter

the 40 reserved oysters

1 tablespoon minced French shallots

1 garlic clove, mashed and minced to produce 1 teaspoon

1 teaspoon chopped fresh thyme

1 cup coarse French-bread crumbs

salt and freshly ground pepper, to taste

Preheat the oven broiler.

In a small skillet over high heat, melt the butter. Add the shallots, garlic, and thyme, and cook for 2 to 3 minutes, or until slightly soft. Add the bread crumbs and stir well to be sure they are evenly coated. Season to taste with salt and pepper.

Reheat the sautéed mushroom mixture from the previous recipe over medium-high heat and stir in the prepared sauce. Bring to a simmer, add the oysters and cook until their edges just begin to curl. Spoon some of the mushroom-and-oyster mixture into the prepared tart-pastry shells, dividing the portions evenly among the pastry shells. Sprinkle the seasoned bread crumbs proportionately among the tarts. Broil until the crumbs are just brown and the sauce is bubbly.

# P&J's Oyster and Crawfish Pasta in Saffron Sauce

*Oysters are delicious with pasta, and the addition of crawfish brings another dimension to that combination. In this recipe, the saffron adds a delicious low note. The delicate sauce really shines when it's served with vermicelli pasta.*

24 shucked fresh oysters

the juices (liquor) from the oysters

2 tablespoons butter

3 green onions, chopped fine

1 small ripe tomato, seeded and diced

1/4 teaspoon garlic powder

1 1/2 teaspoons onion powder

1 pinch cayenne pepper

3 cups heavy cream

pinch of saffron threads

8 ounces cooked crawfish tails

salt and pepper, to taste

1/4 pound vermicelli pasta

**YIELD: 6 servings**

Strain the oyster liquor to remove grit and set aside.

Place the oysters and their liquor in a small saucepan over medium-low heat and cook just until the edges of the oysters just begin to curl, about 3 or 4 minutes. Pour off and discard the oyster liquor. Reserve the oysters until serving time.

In a large sauté pan, melt the butter over medium-low heat. Add and sauté the green onions and tomatoes with the garlic powder, onion powder and cayenne for about 5 minutes, stirring frequently.

Add 1/2 teaspoon of salt to a large pot of water and bring to a boil to cook the vermicelli.

While the pasta is cooking, stir the cream and saffron into the vegetable mixture and increase the heat to medium-high. Stir constantly until the liquids are slightly thickened. Lower the heat to medium-low, season the sauce with salt and pepper to taste and add the oysters and crawfish tails. Cook until the seafood is heated through, about 2 or 3 minutes.

Quickly drain the vermicelli and serve with the sauce.

# Oysters Bordelaise

## TUJAGUE'S

*A simple classic from New Orleans' second oldest restaurant. Serve with hot, crispy French bread and a fresh green salad for a satisfying meal.*

24 shucked fresh oysters

the juices (liquor) from the oysters

4 servings fettuccine

1 tablespoon olive oil

8 tablespoons (1 stick) butter

1/2 cup mushroom slices, 1/4-inch-thick

6 garlic cloves, minced

2 green onions, chopped

2 tablespoons finely chopped parsley, for garnish

**YIELD: 4 to 6 servings**

Strain the oyster juices (the "liquor") into a small bowl to remove grit. Set the liquor and the oysters aside.

Fill a large pot halfway with water and bring it to a boil. Add the fettuccine and cook it according to package directions or until al dente. Drain the fettuccine in a colander or strainer, return it to the empty pot and toss it well with the olive oil.

While preparing the bordelaise sauce, keep the pasta warm in the pot over the lowest possible heat, stirring frequently to prevent it from scorching.

In a large, deep skillet or a Dutch oven over a medium heat, melt the butter and sauté the sliced mushrooms for 4 to 5 minutes, or until almost done; they will continue cooking during the next step. Add the oyster liquor, green onion and garlic to the skillet or pot and cook over medium heat until the edges of the oysters just begin to curl, about 3 to 4 minutes. Remove from heat.

To serve, divide the fettuccine among four pasta bowls or large soup bowls. Ladle the oysters and the bordelaise over the pasta. Garnish each serving with chopped parsley. Serve with warm French bread and a green salad.

# Oysters and Fettuccine Bacco

## CHEF CHRIS MONTERO AND RALPH BRENNAN, BACCO

*Pasta with seafood in a sauce has become a very familiar combination in New Orleans and the rest of South Louisiana. The pairing apparently came about with the realization that pasta could be substituted for rice, which has been the starch found more frequently in the region's seafood dishes.*

*Some of the smoked tomatoes will be used in preparing the Alfredo sauce recipe. An additional amount will go into the sauce during the final steps of the recipe under "Oysters and fettuccine." This is to give additional texture appeal to the finished dish.*

*Note: Preparing this recipe requires a stove-top smoker.*

### SMOKED TOMATOES

*The tomatoes may be prepared up to two days in advance.*

1 1/2 cups fine hickory-wood chips

2 3/4 pounds (4 or 5 large) vine-ripened tomatoes

**YIELD: 6 servings**

Soak the hickory chips in water for at least 4 hours.

Place the smoker on the stove top. Scatter the wet wood chips evenly over the bottom of the space designed to hold the chips, but don't turn the burner on yet.

Core the tomatoes.

When using the smoker, follow the manufacturer's directions and smoke the tomatoes until they are smoked light to medium and the skins have split. (The cooking time will vary, depending on the smoker.)

Smoke the tomatoes over high heat until a good amount of smoke escapes when you open a small vent, about 10 minutes. Close the vent, then reduce heat to medium and continue smoking until the tomato skins are lightly colored from the smoke and have split, about 20 minutes more. Remove from heat.

Very carefully (so you don't burn yourself from the steam) remove the smoker lid and transfer the tomatoes to a platter to cool.

Drain the tomatoes just before using, leaving them dripping wet. Once the tomatoes are cool, peel and chop the pulp. You should have 3 to 4 cups of chopped pulp and juice.

Measure out 1 3/4 cups of the tomatoes and juice and refrigerate them for adding to the Alfredo sauce. Measure out and refrigerate another 1/2 cup of the tomatoes and juice for finishing the oysters and fettuccine dish.

### ALFREDO SAUCE

2 yolks from large eggs

1 3/4 cups heavy cream

4 1/2 ounces grated Parmigiano-Reggiano cheese

1 3/4 cups peeled and chopped smoked tomatoes, from the recipe above

Place the egg yolks in a large heat-proof mixing bowl and lightly beat with a metal whisk. Set aside.

In a heavy, 2 1/2-quart saucepan heat together the cream and Parmigiano-Reggiano cheese over low heat for 5 minutes, whisking almost constantly. Increase the heat to high and continue cooking, whisking constantly, until the mixture is fairly smooth, about 1 minute. Remove from heat.

*(recipe for Oysters and Fettuccine on next page)*

1/4 teaspoon salt, or to taste

1/4 teaspoon freshly ground black pepper, or to taste

Very gradually add the hot cream and cheese mixture to the egg yolks, whisking constantly. Stir in the reserved 1 3/4 cups of smoked tomatoes.

Process this entire mixture in a blender to a smooth purée. If the sauce is thin (it should be the consistency of fairly thick heavy cream), return it to the saucepan and cook over medium heat just until it thickens, whisking constantly.

Remove the sauce from heat and season it with salt and pepper to taste.

If the sauce was prepared ahead, let it cool and then refrigerate it in a covered container.

There should be some sauce left over. It may be put to other uses, such as being reheated gently in a double boiler over hot (not simmering) water, then tossed with cooked pasta and topped with grated Parmigiano-Reggiano cheese.

## OYSTERS AND FETTUCCINE

30 shucked fresh oysters

3 tablespoons olive oil, divided

6 ounces pancetta, cut in 1/4-inch slices, and slices cut in 1/4-inch cubes

salted water for cooking fettuccine

1 pound dry fettuccine

3 tablespoons minced garlic

1/4 to 1/2 teaspoon crushed red pepper

1/2 cup peeled and chopped smoked tomatoes, drained

3 cups Alfredo sauce, from recipe above

1/2 teaspoon salt, plus to taste

6 teaspoons very finely sliced green onions (green parts only), for garnish

Strain the oyster juices (the "liquor") into a container to remove grit and refrigerate or freeze for future use. Set the oysters aside.

In a heavy, 12-inch sauté pan, combine 1 tablespoon olive oil and the pancetta. Cook over medium-low heat until the fat renders out of the meat but the meat itself is only slightly crispy, 10 to 12 minutes, stirring occasionally. Remove from heat.

Meanwhile, heat the salted water and cook the fettuccine until it is almost al dente. Drain well and rinse with cool water. Drain again.

Place the fettuccine in a large mixing bowl and toss with 2 tablespoons of the olive oil, mixing to coat all the strands with oil. Cover the bowl with a double thickness of damp paper towels and set aside at room temperature.

Once the pancetta has been rendered, drain all except 2 tablespoons of the fat from the pan. If the rendering process did not produce 2 tablespoons of fat, add enough of the remaining 1 tablespoon of olive oil to the pan to make 2 tablespoons.

Place the pan over high heat. Add the garlic, crushed red pepper and reserved 1/2 cup of smoked tomatoes. Sauté for one minute, stirring constantly.

Reduce the heat to medium-low and add the 3 cups of Alfredo sauce and 1/2 teaspoon of salt. Cook until the sauce is heated through, about 2 minutes, stirring frequently. Add the oysters and cook just until they are plump and their edges just begin to curl, about 2 minutes.

Add the drained fettuccine to the pan, tossing with tongs to coat well with sauce. Continue cooking until the fettuccine is heated through, about 1 minute more, tossing almost constantly. Remove from heat and season with more salt if needed.

To serve, divide the oysters and fettuccine among six warmed, individual pasta bowls. Garnish each with 1 teaspoon green onions.

# Oyster Pilaf

## CHARLIE MALACHIAS, CAFÉ MASPERO,

*Café Maspero has been a landmark since the early days of New Orleans. Formerly it was La Casa de los Marinos, a legendary French Quarter watering hole frequented by Cuban sailors.*

36 fresh shucked oysters

the juices (liquor) from the oysters

8 tablespoons (1 stick) unsalted butter

1 medium onion, minced

1 garlic clove, mashed

2 celery stalks, minced

2 peeled Roma tomatoes, finely chopped

1 cup raw rice

1/2 teaspoon salt

1/2 teaspoon freshly ground black pepper

1 3/4 cup chicken broth

1/2 cup milk

**YIELD: 6 to 12 servings**

Strain the oyster liquor to remove grit and set aside.

In a deep frying pan or skillet, melt the butter over medium-low heat and sauté the onion, garlic and celery until they are soft. Add the chopped tomatoes and cook for 5 minutes. Add the rice, salt and pepper and stir.

In a saucepan bring the chicken broth and oyster liquor to a boil. Add the rice mixture. Reduce heat to low, cover and simmer the liquid for 12 minutes, or until it is almost absorbed and the rice is cooked.

Add the oysters and lightly stir in the milk. Continue cooking until the oysters just begin to curl, about 5 minutes. Remove from heat and let stand covered for 5 minutes before serving.

# P&J's Pasta Aglio Olio

## BLAKE SUNSERI

*Pasta and oysters are natural companions with dozens of ways to add sauces and cheeses to the recipe for an original creation.*

24 shucked fresh oysters

1 pound angel hair pasta

4 tablespoons extra-virgin olive oil

2 tablespoons finely chopped garlic

2 teaspoons chile paste

1 cup pasta water

salt and freshly ground black pepper, to taste

1 tablespoon finely chopped parsley

4 tablespoons grated Pecorino Romano cheese

**YIELD: 4 to 6 servings**

Drain the juices (the "liquor") from the oysters with a strainer to remove grit, collecting the juices in a container and refrigerate or freeze them for future use.

In a large pot of boiling, salted water, cook the pasta about 8 minutes, or until "al dente." Drain the pasta, reserving 1 cup of the pasta water.

In a large sauté pan, heat 2 tablespoons of the olive oil and then add the garlic. Stir until the garlic is softened and the oil begins to bubble.

Add the oysters and cook just until edges curl, about 2 minutes. Add the chile paste, 1/2 cup of the pasta water, a pinch of salt, a twist of pepper and the parsley. Drain the pasta, then add it to the pan and toss it with the olive-oil mixture.

Add the remaining 1/2 cup of pasta water, the remaining 2 tablespoons of olive oil, and 2 tablespoons of the Pecorino Romano cheese. Toss again, and transfer to a warmed serving bowl. Evenly scatter the remaining 2 tablespoons of cheese over the pasta and serve immediately.

# Poached Oysters and Pasta

## CHEF TOM WOLFE, WOLFE'S

*Placed in individual sushi plates, this recipe makes entertaining bites. Served in larger portions and dishes, it is a spectacular appetizer or even entrée.*

40 shucked fresh oysters

1/4 cup oyster liquor

3 cups cooked angel hair pasta

4 teaspoons butter

4 teaspoons minced French shallot

3 teaspoons chopped garlic

8 tablespoons chopped parsley

1 cup dry white wine

2 cups heavy cream

1 teaspoon Herbsaint, Pernod or other anisette liqueur

salt and freshly ground white pepper, to taste

parsley sprigs, for garnish

grated Parmigiano-Reggiano cheese

**YIELD: 40 bites, 12 appetizers or 4 entrées**

Strain the oyster juices (the "liquor") into a measuring container to remove grit. Reserve 1/4 cup of the liquor. Refrigerate or freeze the remaining liquor for future use. Set the oysters and liquor aside.

Cook the angel-hair pasta in boiling water until al dente. Drain the pasta in a colander or strainer and set aside.

In a 2-quart saucepan, melt the butter over high heat and add the shallot, garlic and parsley. Reduce heat to medium-high and sauté the vegetables until they are soft, about 3 minutes.

Add the wine to deglaze the pan. Allow the vegetables and wine to simmer until the liquid is reduced to 2/3 of the original amount.

When the liquid is reduced, add the cream and bring to a boil. Add the raw oysters and the oyster liquor to the reduced liquid. Cook the oysters until the edges just begin to curl, approximately 2 1/2 to 3 minutes. Season with the anisette liqueur and the salt and pepper. Remove from heat.

Spoon the cooked angel-hair pasta into pasta bowls or shallow soup bowls. Top each serving with some of the oysters and white-wine garlic cream. Garnish with parsley sprigs and grated Parmigiano-Reggiano cheese, to taste. Serve immediately.

# Oysters and Spaghetti

**FELIX'S**

*Felix's is well known for its raw oysters on the half-shell and fresh seafood fried the traditional New Orleans way. Here is a simple and satisfying version of an old New Orleans favorite. Founded in the early 1900s, Felix's is another family-owned-and-operated establishment.*

48 shucked fresh oysters

the juices (liquor) from the oysters

8 tablespoons (1 stick) butter

1/2 cup diced French shallots

8 garlic cloves, minced

1/2 cup chopped parsley

1 pound cooked spaghetti

salt and pepper to taste

grated Parmigiano-Reggiano cheese, for garnish

**YIELD: 4 to 6 servings**

Strain the oyster liquor to remove grit and set aside.

Place the butter in a saucepan over medium heat until melted. Add the shallots, garlic and parsley and sauté until softened. Add the oysters and their liquor and sauté until the edges of the oysters just begin to curl. Add salt and pepper to taste. Keep the sauce warm while you cook the spaghetti.

In a pot of boiling water, cook the spaghetti until the strands are al dente. Drain in a colander or strainer. Place the pasta and the sauce with the oysters in a large bowl and toss to coat the pasta evenly.

Divide the spaghetti and oysters among 4 to 6 pasta bowls or shallow soup bowls. Garnish with the grated cheese and serve immediately.

# P&J's Oyster-and-Shrimp-Topped Risotto

*A creamy risotto is the perfect foil for the duo of oysters and shrimp fresh from the coastal waters of Louisiana.*

24 shucked fresh oysters

8 tablespoons (1 stick) butter, divided

1 cup chopped white or yellow onion

3 cups arborio rice

5 cups chicken broth or stock (page 210)

2 teaspoons salt

2 teaspoons freshly ground pepper

1 3/4 pounds raw medium
(31 to 35 per pound) shrimp, shelled

2 teaspoons garlic, minced or pressed

8 ounces white or mixed mushrooms,
cleaned and chopped

2 tablespoons brandy

2 cups shrimp stock, fish stock, or
bottled clam juice

1 cup heavy cream

2 cups baby spinach leaves, stems removed,
washed and dried

1 tablespoon chopped parsley

**YIELD: 6 to 8 main-course servings**

Strain the oyster juices (the "liquor") into a container to remove grit and refrigerate or freeze for future use.

Warm the chicken broth over medium-high heat in a large saucepan.

In a separate large saucepan over medium heat, begin warming 6 tablespoons of the butter in a separate large saucepan. Add and sauté the onion until translucent. Add the rice to the onion, increase the heat to medium and sauté for 2 minutes. Meanwhile begin adding the warm chicken broth 1 cup at a time, stirring constantly. Add more broth as the amount in the pan is absorbed.

Continue until the rice is tender, but al dente (still has a little bite). The consistency should be creamy. Stir in 2 teaspoons each of salt and pepper, or to taste. Cover the pan and set the sauce aside

In a large skillet, melt the remaining butter over medium heat. Add and sauté the shrimp, garlic and mushrooms until the shrimp are starting to turn pink. Flambé the mixture by pouring the brandy into a warmed ladle and carefully igniting it with a kitchen match. Again, carefully, add the brandy to the skillet and allow it to burn off.

Add the shrimp stock, increase the heat to medium-high and bring the liquid to a boil. Let it reduce for 2 to 3 minutes. Stir in the cream, bring back to a boil, and let the liquid reduce for another 2 minutes, stirring frequently. Add the oysters and spinach, and cook for 1 minute more.

At serving time, spoon some of the rice onto a serving plate, then top it with some of the creamy seafood mixture. Sprinkle each serving with a pinch or two of chopped parsley.

# P&J's Oyster and Mushroom Pie

*Oysters and mushrooms are cheerful companions. This recipe does not call for a pastry crust, and relies instead on a topping of seasoned bread crumbs.*

48 fresh shucked oysters

the juices (liquor) from the oysters

about 1 cup heavy cream

5 tablespoons unsalted butter

8 ounces mushrooms, cleaned and sliced

2 tablespoons all-purpose flour

1/2 teaspoon worcestershire sauce

1 teaspoon fresh lemon juice

salt and freshly ground black pepper, to taste

pinch of cayenne pepper

1 cup soft, fresh bread crumbs

**YIELD: 12 appetizer servings or 6 main-course servings**

Strain the oyster liquor to remove grit. Measure the oyster liquor and add enough cream to make 1 1/2 cups. Set the liquor and the oysters aside.

In a saucepan, warm 2 tablespoons of the butter over medium-high heat. Add and sauté the mushrooms for about 3 minutes, stirring, until lightly browned. Transfer the mushrooms to a plate and set aside.

Preheat the oven to 425°F.

Grease a 9-inch Pyrex pie plate with 1 tablespoon of the butter and set aside.

Reduce the heat under the pan used to cook the mushrooms. Add 1 tablespoon of the remaining butter to the pan. When the butter has melted, add the flour. Stir to make a paste and cook, still stirring, for 1 minute. Gradually add the mixture of oyster liquor and cream, and bring to a gentle simmer. Stir constantly until the liquid thickens, about 3 minutes more.

Add the reserved mushrooms and the oysters (with any accumulated juices), worcestershire sauce, lemon juice, salt, and the black and cayenne pepper. Stir and simmer an additional minute or two, until everything is well blended.

Pour the mixture into the pie plate, sprinkle with the bread crumbs, and dot evenly with the remaining tablespoon of butter. Bake uncovered, until bubbling and golden, about 10 minutes. Let stand for 5 minutes before serving.

# P&J's Oyster Quiche

*Brunch or a Sunday evening supper is a perfect time to present this unusual dish. Serve it with a green salad and French bread and it is an entire meal. Versatile, it may also be cooked in a square baking dish, cooled and cut into 2 inch cubes and served as a canapé.*

24 shucked fresh oysters

the juices ("liquor") from the oysters

1 tablespoon butter

1/2 cup chopped mushrooms

1/3 cup chopped green onions

1/4 cup chopped green sweet pepper

2 eggs

1/2 teaspoon salt

1 teaspoon dried basil or 3 large fresh basil leaves, finely chopped

1 cup whole milk

1/4 cup chopped parsley

salt, to taste

1 1/2 cups grated Swiss cheese

dash of garlic powder

1 (9-inch) pie shell, slightly browned

1 teaspoon paprika

**YIELD: 6 to 8 servings**

Preheat the oven to 350°F.

Strain the oyster juices (the "liquor") into small bowl to remove grit. Pour the liquor into a skillet, add the oysters and bring the liquid to a simmer over medium heat, Cook for 10 minutes, until the oyster edges begin to curl, then remove the oysters with a slotted spoon and drain them well. Cut the oysters into quarters and set them aside.

Discard the remaining oyster liquor. Then, in the same skillet, heat the butter and sauté the mushrooms, green onion and sweet pepper until they are soft. Add the quartered oysters and mix them with the vegetables.

In a medium-size bowl, whisk the eggs. Add the basil, parsley, salt to taste and milk. Beat the mixture until foamy then blend in the grated cheese.

Ladle the oyster-and-vegetable mixture evenly into the pie shell. Slowly pour in the egg-and-cheese mixture, allowing it to cover the oysters.

Sprinkle the paprika on top of the quiche and bake until the cheese is lightly browned and the quiche is firmly set, about 50 minutes. Cool the quiche for 10 minutes before serving.

# Gratins, Stuffings and Dressings

*Stuffing is a necessity in these parts. We use it to enhance any manner of meals, and when prepared as a casserole, it is the meal. As for gratins, they also can contain oysters but also rely on other ingredient combinations, often creamy, to carry the flavors along, blending texture and taste in exciting and unusual ways.*

# Oyster Gratin with Horseradish

## CHEF JOHN BESH, LÜKE

*Lüke is John Besh's tribute to the brasseries that are found in virtually every Paris neighborhood. The menus, like those in each of Besh's four restaurants, are filled with full-flavored and imaginative treatments of traditional French and New Orleans dishes.*

24 shucked fresh oysters

1/4 cup butter

1/4 cup all-purpose flour

1/2 onion, sliced

1 garlic clove, crushed

2 cups milk

1 clove

1 bay leaf

1/2 cup prepared horseradish

salt and freshly ground black pepper, to taste

1/3 cup bread crumbs

1/3 cup grated Parmigiano-Reggiano cheese

1/3 cup olive oil

1 teaspoon crushed red-pepper flakes

**YIELD: 6 to 8 servings**

Strain the oyster juices (the "liquor") into a container to remove grit and refrigerate or freeze for future use. Place the oysters in a bowl and set aside.

Preheat the oven to 450°

In a large saucepan melt the butter over medium high heat and add the flour. Combine the butter and flour and stir with a whisk. Continue stirring for 5 minutes, allowing the blond roux to cook, but not brown. Add the onion and garlic, lower the heat to medium and cook, stirring continuously, until the onions are translucent.

Add the milk, continuing to stir, and raise heat to high. Bring the sauce to a boil, then lower heat to low. Add the clove and bay leaf, and allow the sauce to simmer for 45 minutes. This is the béchamel sauce.

Remove the sauce from heat and stir in the horseradish. Season to taste with salt and black pepper. Strain the sauce through a fine sieve and allow it to cool.

Season the oysters with salt and pepper and place them in the bottom of a casserole dish.

Pour the béchamel sauce evenly over the oysters.

In a bowl, combine the bread crumbs, oil, Parmigiano-Reggiano cheese and red-pepper flakes. Sprinkle the mixture generously over the oysters. Bake for about 15 minutes, or until golden brown.

# P&J's Oysters and Artichokes

*For a company dinner or a party, or to treat your family very well, this recipe combines wonderful ingredients in a melange of compatible flavors. You'll be asked for the recipe, and whether or not to keep it to yourself is completely up to you.*

36 shucked fresh oysters

the juices (liquor) from the oysters

8 tablespoons (1 stick) unsalted butter

1/3 pound button mushrooms

2 (10-ounce) packages frozen artichoke hearts, thawed and drained

3/4 cup dry white wine

2 bunches green onions, trimmed and finely chopped

1/2 cup all-purpose flour

1/2 cup finely chopped parsley

2 tablespoons fresh lemon juice

1/8 teaspoon dried thyme

salt and freshly ground black pepper, to taste

1 teaspoon cayenne pepper

1 lemon, halved and thinly sliced, for garnish

parsley sprigs, for garnish

crusty French bread, for serving

**YIELD: 12 appetizers**

Preheat the oven to 350°F.

Strain the oyster liquor to remove grit and set aside. Cut the artichoke hearts in quarters and the mushrooms in 1/4-inch slices. Grease ten 4-ounce ramekins.

In a saucepan, melt 4 tablespoons (1/2 stick) of the butter over medium-high heat. Add the mushrooms to the melted butter, and sauté until tender. Add the artichokes and stir occasionally until heated through. Divide the mixture evenly among the ramekins and set aside.

Pour the oyster liquor into the same saucepan and cook the oysters over medium-high heat for 2 to 3 minutes, just until the edges begin to curl. Remove the pan from the heat and drain the oysters through a sieve into a small bowl to reserve their liquor. Set the oysters aside and pour the liquor into a measuring cup. Add the wine to the oyster liquor, and add water until the wine and liquor mixture is 1 3/4 cups.

In a separate, large sauté pan, melt the remaining 4 tablespoons of butter over medium-high heat, and slowly add the flour. Using a whisk, cook just until the butter and flour are incorporated. Add the green onions. Slowly stir in the oyster-liquor-and-wine mixture, and then the chopped parsley, lemon juice, thyme, salt and pepper. Stirring constantly, cook over medium high heat. When the mixture thickens, stir in the cooked oysters. Then spoon the mixture over the artichokes and mushrooms in the ramekins. Sprinkle the tops evenly with the cayenne pepper.

Bake for 8 minutes, or until bubbly. Before serving, garnish each ramekin with a sprig of parsley and a half-slice of lemon. Serve with thick slices of French bread on the side, for dipping.

# Oysters Marie Laveau

## CHEF JOHN FOLSE

*This recipe gets its name from the woman who reigned as the queen of voodoo in 19th century New Orleans. Laveau used magical charms and potions in her exotic religious rites. The only supernatural aspect of this dish is its awesome flavor. Chef Folse is an acclaimed author and entrepreneur, devoting himself to a great many civic and charitable activities.*

### OYSTERS

36 shucked fresh oysters

the juices (liquor) from the oysters

3 tablespoons butter

1 teaspoon minced garlic

1 teaspoon chopped parsley

1/2 liquid ounce anisette liqueur,
Pernod or Herbsaint

### SAUCE

8 tablespoons (1 stick) butter

1/2 cup diced yellow onion

1/4 cup diced celery

2 tablespoons minced garlic

1/4 cup sliced green onions

1/2 cup lump crab meat, or
1/2 cup chopped cooked shrimp

2 1/2 tablespoons flour

3 cups heavy whipping cream

1/8 cup dry white wine

the reduced liquid from the oysters

the reserved oyster liquor

1/2 teaspoon ground nutmeg

1/4 cup diced red sweet pepper

1/4 cup diced yellow sweet pepper

salt, to taste

freshly ground black pepper, to taste

grated Parmigiano-Reggiano cheese,
for topping, optional

**YIELD: 6 servings**

Strain the oyster liquor in a bowl to remove grit. Set aside the oysters and the liquor.

In a heavy-bottomed sauté pan, melt the butter over medium-high heat. Stir in the garlic and parsley and sauté 2 minutes. Add the oysters and cook until the edges just begin to curl, but do not overcook. Deglaze the pan with anisette liqueur and cook 1 minute. Remove the oysters with a slotted spoon and reduce the liquid by half. Reserve the oysters and the liquid.

Preheat the oven to 375°F.

In a 1-quart, heavy-bottomed saucepan, melt the butter over medium-high heat. Add the yellow onion, celery, garlic and green onion and sauté 3 minutes. Stirring constantly, add the crab meat or shrimp and sauté 1 minute. Whisk in the flour to produce a white roux, then whisk in the cream and wine. Bring to a low boil, stirring constantly as the mixture thickens.

Pour in the reserved liquid from the oysters and reserved oyster liquor. Reduce heat to simmer and cook 10 to 15 minutes, adding hot water if the sauce becomes too thick.

Add the nutmeg and sweet pepper, then season with salt and pepper.

Place 6 oysters in each of six au gratin dishes and top each with a generous serving of sauce. If desired, sprinkle Parmigiano-Reggiano cheese on top of each dish. Bake until bubbly. Serve with garlic croutons or warm, crusty French bread.

# Oyster, Bacon and Eggplant Gratin

## CHEF DONALD LINK, HERBSAINT

*Donald Link's accolades include a James Beard Award for Best Chef in the South. He earned it by creating big flavors drawn from his roots in the Louisiana bayou country. He followed his success in New Orleans at Herbsaint with Cochon, a larger, more casual eatery specializing in many parts of the porker.*

15 shucked fresh oysters

4 slices thick-sliced raw bacon, 1/4-inch dice

2 tablespoons olive oil, divided

1/2 cup eggplant in 1/2-inch dice

salt and freshly ground pepper, to taste

6 tablespoons softened butter, divided

1 or 2 finely chopped garlic cloves

juice and zest from 1 lemon

2 teaspoons chopped parsley, divided

3 tablespoons bread crumbs

3 tablespoons Parmigiano-Reggiano cheese

**YIELD: 8 to 12 appetizer servings**

Strain the oyster juices (the "liquor") into a container to remove grit and refrigerate or freeze the liquor for future use. Set the oysters aside.

Preheat the oven to 475°F.

In a skillet, render the diced bacon in 1 tablespoon of olive oil until cooked through. Remove the bacon pieces with a slotted spoon. Do not remove the fat from the skillet.

In the fat, sauté the eggplant pieces over medium heat until they are cooked through. Season with salt and pepper.

Combine 4 tablespoons of the softened butter, garlic, lemon juice, lemon zest and 1 teaspoon of the parsley. Season with pinches of salt and pepper. Mash the butter and seasonings together with a fork until all are thoroughly mixed.

Combine the bread crumbs, Parmigiano-Reggiano, the remaining 1 teaspoon of parsley and 1 tablespoon of olive oil. Season with salt and pepper. Set aside.

In the pre-heated oven, warm an 8-inch cast-iron skillet or a baking pan of similar dimensions so the heat will be evenly distributed when the mixture is placed in the oven. When the skillet or pan is warm, remove it from the oven. In it, evenly distribute the raw oysters, eggplant and bacon in one layer. Using a spoon, dot the top of the mixture with pieces of the remaining 2 tablespoons of softened butter. Sprinkle the seasoned bread crumbs over the oysters, eggplant and bacon.

Bake for about 5 minutes, or until the bread crumbs are lightly browned.

# Oysters Gabie

## CHEFS GREG AND MARY SONNIER

*Greg and his wife Mary are both at home in restaurant kitchens. They named this dish for their daughter Gabrielle, who is also the namesake of the couple's first restaurant.*

16 to 20 shucked fresh oysters

the juices (liquor) from the oysters

1 lemon, halved

4 tablespoons olive oil, divided

2 large raw artichokes, stems removed

4 ounces pancetta, finely diced

1 tablespoon butter

1/4 cup chopped green onions, white part only

1 tablespoon minced garlic

2 tablespoons minced parsley

salt and freshly ground black pepper, to taste

1/4 cup plus 2 tablespoons dry bread crumbs

1/4 cup plus 2 tablespoons grated Parmigiano-Reggiano cheese

hollandaise sauce (page (216)

**YIELD: 4 servings**

Strain the oyster liquor into a small bowl to remove grit. Set aside both the liquor and the oysters.

Preheat the oven to 450°F.

Place the lemon halves and 2 tablespoons of the olive oil in a large pot of boiling water. Add the artichokes and cook them until tender, about 20 minutes. Drain the artichokes and allow them to cool.

Pull the leaves from the artichokes and scrape the flesh from the larger leaves with a spoon into a small bowl. Pull the remaining leaves and use a spoon to dig out the fuzzy, inedible "choke" at the bottoms of the artichokes, exposing the tender, fleshy "hearts." Trim the hearts and dice them. Set the diced hearts and the scraped artichoke flesh.

Begin making the dressing. In a medium sauté pan or skillet, heat 1 more tablespoon of the olive oil and cook the pancetta until brown. Add the remaining 1 tablespoon of oil and the butter. Sauté the green onions, garlic and parsley until tender, about 3 to 4 minutes. Add the diced artichokes and lemon juice. If the dressing seems dry, add some oyster liquor to moisten it. Sauté the mixture for about 2 minutes. Adjust the seasonings and remove the dressing from heat. Add 1/4 cup of the bread crumbs and 1/4 cup of the cheese and toss lightly.

Place 4 or 5 oysters into small individual casseroles or ramekins. Top the oysters with the artichoke dressing and sprinkle with the remaining cheese and bread crumbs. Bake until browned, 10 to 15 minutes. Serve with a drizzle of hollandaise sauce over the dressing.

# Oyster Gratin

## BEGUE'S, THE ROYAL SONESTA

*The Royal Sonesta's restaurant is named in honor of Madame Elizabeth Bégué, the legendary cook who founded a restaurant of that name with her husband in 1863 on Decatur Street in New Orleans. This recipe is an unusual creation whose flavor is blessed with fennel.*

### ARTICHOKE BÉCHAMEL SAUCE

Yield: 1 1/2 to 2 cups

2 tablespoons unsalted butter

2 tablespoons all-purpose flour

1 cup milk

1/4 cup heavy cream

1 whole bay leaf

1/4 cup Parmigiano-Reggiano cheese

1 teaspoon fresh lemon juice

1/2 teaspoon lemon zest

1/4 cup olive oil

4 cooked artichoke bottoms (or 8 ounces frozen artichoke hearts), in 1/4-inch dice

1 tablespoon minced garlic

1 tablespoon minced French shallot

2 sprigs fresh thyme

1/4 cup Herbsaint, or other anisette liqueur

salt and freshly ground white pepper, to taste

**YIELD: 4 servings**

In a 2-quart saucepan, heat the butter over moderate heat and whisk in the flour. Continue whisking until the mixture thickens to a blond roux. Add the milk, cream and bay leaf, and bring the mixture to a simmer. Whisk in the Parmigiano-Reggiano, lemon juice and lemon zest.

In another 2-quart saucepan, heat the olive oil. Add the artichoke bottoms, garlic, shallot and fresh thyme and cook until the garlic and shallots are soft. Deglaze the saucepan with the Herbsaint or other anisette liqueur and reduce the liquid by 3/4.

Stir the béchamel sauce in the other saucepan into the sautéed artichoke bottoms and season to taste with salt and white pepper. Cook on low heat for at least 20 minutes.

*(see recipe for Gratin Ingredients on next page)*

## GRATIN INGREDIENTS

2 packed cups raw spinach leaves torn into
bite-size pieces

1 1/2 to 2 cups artichoke béchamel sauce
from previous recipe

2 tablespoons extra-virgin olive oil

1 fennel bulb, sliced and julienned into
matchstick pieces

1/2 teaspoon minced garlic

1 teaspoon minced French shallots

20 shucked fresh oysters

pinch cayenne pepper

dash worcestershire sauce

juice from 1/2 lemon

dash Herbsaint or other anisette liqueur

2 tablespoons panko bread crumbs
mixed with 2 tablespoons grated
Parmigiano-Reggiano cheese

2 tablespoons unsalted butter

fennel fronds, for garnish

1 lemon, cut into quarters

Preheat the oven to 450°F or preheat the oven broiler.

Blanch the spinach as follows: Prepare a large bowl of ice water by adding ice cubes to the bath and set aside. Submerge the torn spinach leaves in a pot of boiling water for 1 minute. With the spinach pieces in the strainer, press them down firmly with a wooden spoon to release as much water as possible. Plunge the spinach into the ice water. Drain thoroughly and set aside. This should produce about 1 cup of blanched spinach.

In a saucepan, combine the artichoke béchamel sauce with the blanched spinach and cook over low to medium heat until everything is heated through. Place the sauce in one 18-to-24-ounce, oven-proof serving dish or divide the sauce into four 4-to-6-ounce gratin dishes that will provide four individual servings.

In a large skillet heat 1 of the 2 tablespoons of olive oil and sauté the fennel-bulb julienned strips, the minced garlic and minced shallot until all are caramelized to a dark brown. Remove them from the skillet and place them on top of the artichoke-and-spinach béchamel in either the large gratin dish or the four smaller ones.

Using the same skillet, heat the second tablespoon of olive oil over medium-low heat. Add the oysters to the skillet and season with the cayenne, worcestershire, lemon and Herbsaint or other anisette liqueur. Gently cook the oysters until their edges begin to curl.

Spoon the cooked oysters onto the layer of caramelized fennel, garlic and shallot. Sprinkle the oysters with the mixture of panko bread crumbs and Parmigiano-Reggiano. Place pieces of the softened butter on top of the bread crumbs and lightly brown the top of the gratin in the 450°F oven or the broiler. Remove the gratin from the oven. Garnish with fennel fronds and lemon quarters.

# Oyster Dressing

## CHEF GUS MARTIN, MURIEL'S JACKSON SQUARE

*The balcony at Muriel's overlooks Jackson Square and the famous apartment buildings erected in the mid-19th century by the Creole Baroness de Pontalba. Some say that ghosts haunt the restaurant. Ghosts, or no ghosts, the memories of glorious meals linger in the dining rooms.*

1 pound (4 sticks) unsalted butter

2 tablespoons minced garlic

1 cup medium-diced green sweet pepper

2 cups medium-diced yellow onion

1 cup medium-diced celery

1 tablespoon dried thyme

4 whole bay leaves

48 shucked fresh oysters, coarsely chopped

9 cups coarse bread crumbs

2 tablespoons salt

1 teaspoon freshly ground black pepper

2 bunches green onions, finely chopped

**YIELD: 3 quarts**

Preheat the oven to 350°F.

Strain the oyster juices (the "liquor") into a container to remove grit and refrigerate or freeze for future use.

In a medium saucepan, melt the butter over medium-high heat. Add the garlic, sweet pepper, yellow onion, celery, thyme and bay leaves. Cook until the garlic, pepper, onion and celery are soft. Reduce heat to medium, add the chopped oysters and cook for 5 minutes. Add the bread crumbs, salt, pepper and green onions. Continue to cook for another 5 to10 minutes over medium heat, stirring occasionally, until the green onions are wilted and the bread crumbs are incorporated.

Place the stuffing in a 2-to-3-quart casserole and bake 20 to 30 minutes, watching carefully, until it is heated through and a golden brown crust forms on top. (The shallower the baking dish the faster the casserole will heat throughout and brown on top.)

# Oyster Dressing

## JERRY AMATO, MOTHER'S RESTAURANT

*Mother's is world-renowned for its hearty po-boys and baked ham, along with such blue-plate specials as red beans and rice and jambalaya. Located in the heart of the New Orleans Central Business District, it's a favorite of judges, workers and visitors who wait in line to share communal tables.*

8 dozen (96) shucked fresh oysters

3 slices raw bacon

1/2 cup olive oil

1/2 cup finely chopped onion

1/2 cup finely chopped green sweet pepper

1/4 cup chopped celery

1 teaspoon salt

1 teaspoon freshly ground black pepper

1 tablespoon garlic powder

1/2 teaspoon dried basil

1/2 teaspoon dried oregano

1 quart chicken stock (page 210)

1/2 cup grated Parmigiano-Reggiano cheese

1 1/2 cups seasoned bread crumbs, divided

1/2 cup chopped green onions

chicken stock or water for additional moisture

**YIELD: 3 quarts**

Strain the oysters over a bowl to remove grit and to separate them from the liquor. Chop the oysters coarsely.

Preheat the oven to 350°F.

Place the oysters and their liquor in a medium-size roasting pan. Set aside.

Fry the bacon slices to a crisp, drain them well on paper towels, and crumble them in a bowl. Set aside.

Heat the olive oil in skillet over medium-high heat. Reduce the heat to medium and sauté the onion, sweet pepper and celery until they are soft and begin to brown. Add the salt, pepper, garlic powder, basil and oregano and stir well. Stir in the chicken stock and bring the liquid to a simmer.

Once the seasoned stock has reached a simmer, pour it with the seasonings into the roasting pan containing the oysters and mix everything well. Mix 3/4 cup of the bread crumbs with the crumbled bacon and combine them thoroughly with the oysters and stock in the roasting pan. Make sure the mixture is still moist by compressing it into a loose ball. If it seems too dry, add a bit more chicken stock or water. Spread the cheese and remaining 3/4 cup of bread crumbs evenly over the dressing. Bake for 20 to 25 minutes, or until nicely browned.

# P&J's Oyster, Sausage and Pecan Dressing

*The addition of sausage and pecans to the Sunseri family's recipe for oyster dressing makes it not only a holiday season treat, but a year-round favorite side dish.*

24 shucked fresh oysters

3/4 pound bulk pork sausage

8 tablespoons (1 stick) butter

3/4 cup finely chopped onion

1/2 cup chopped green sweet pepper

1/2 cup chopped celery

2 large eggs

1 teaspoon poultry seasoning

3/4 cup pecans

5 cups white bread cubes

5 cups crumbled corn bread

salt and freshly ground black pepper, to taste

1 to 1 1/2 cups chicken stock (page 210)

**YIELD: 2 quarts**

Preheat the oven to 350°F.

In a large skillet break up the sausage with a fork and cook it until the pieces are almost browned. Add the oysters and toss them with the sausage until the oyster edges begin to curl. Drain the sausage and oysters, and reserve 2 tablespoons of sausage drippings. Place the sausage and oysters in a bowl and set aside.

In the same pan, melt the butter and add the onion, sweet pepper and celery. Cook over medium heat, stirring, until the vegetables are soft, about 5 minutes, Set aside.

In a large bowl beat the eggs with the poultry seasoning, salt and pepper. Add the bread cubes and corn bread to the egg mixture, tossing until the cubes are nicely coated. Add the cooked onion, sweet pepper and celery, the sausage and oysters, the reserved drippings, and the pecans, and mix thoroughly again. Finally, add the chicken stock and mix to moisten the dressing.

Place the dressing in a 2-quart casserole. Bake until crisp and light brown on top, about 30 to 45 minutes. (Any leftover cornbread is a delightful snack.)

# Stocks,
# Sauces and
# Seasonings

*Lagniappe means a little something extra.*
*What would oysters be without the savory*
*accoutrements of herbs, spices and sauces?*

# Stocks

The most important sauces begin with a good stock. If time or convenience is a consideration, a variety of good-quality stocks and demi-glaces may be purchased frozen, canned or boxed. Any leftover stock can be divided among 1- or 2-cup containers and frozen.

## French Court-Bouillon

4 quarts water

1 carrot, sliced

3 stalks celery, sliced

1/2 small white onion, sliced

3 whole bay leaves

3 cloves

1/2 teaspoon whole black peppercorns

2 teaspoons salt

**YIELD: About 4 quarts**

*This is the secret ingredient in many French and Creole dishes. It is a superb poaching liquid for fish, chicken or sweetbreads. It will keep in the refrigerator for up to a week.*

Combine all ingredients in a pot and bring to a boil over high heat. Boil for about 30 minutes to allow the flavors to develop. Strain into a large bowl through a colander lined with cheesecloth or a fine sieve.

## Chicken Stock

2 pounds raw or cooked chicken bones, including meat pieces

1 pound raw chicken legs, including meat

1 pound yellow onions, coarsely chopped

1/4 pound carrots, coarsely chopped

1/2 tablespoons whole black peppercorns

4 whole bay leaves

1 head garlic, cut in half

1/2 tablespoon dried thyme

1 gallon chilled water

**YIELD: About 3 quarts**

Wash the bones and chicken legs in several changes of water and chop them coarsely with a meat cleaver or a heavy, sturdy knife. Place all ingredients in a stock pot and bring to a boil, then lower the heat so the liquid simmers gently. (Do not allow the stock to boil rapidly, or it will turn cloudy.)

Cook the stock, partially covered, skimming occasionally to remove foam and solids, for about 3 hours. Strain into a large bowl through a colander lined with cheesecloth or a fine sieve.

## Fish or Seafood Stock

2 pounds fish trimmings, shrimp, lobster
or crawfish shells, or small,
cleaned "gumbo (small) crabs,"
all rinsed and coarsely chopped

1/2 pound onions, coarsely chopped

1/2 pound leeks, coarsely chopped

1/2 pound celery, coarsely chopped

4 whole bay leaves

1 teaspoon fresh dried thyme

1 1/2 teaspoons whole white peppercorns

1 head garlic, cut in half

4 quarts chilled water

**YIELD: 4 quarts**

Place all ingredients in a stock pot and bring to a boil, then lower the heat so the liquid simmers gently. (Do not allow the stock to boil rapidly, or it will turn cloudy.)

Cook the stock, partially covered, skimming occasionally to remove foam and solids, for about 45 minutes. Strain into a large bowl through a colander lined with cheesecloth or a fine sieve.

## Veal or Beef Stock

2 pounds raw veal or beef bones

3 tablespoons salt

8 quarts water

2 2/3 cups sliced yellow onions

2 cups sliced carrots

1 cup sliced leeks

1 2/3 cups sliced celery

1 cup chopped flat leaf parsley

1 teaspoon dried thyme

2 whole bay leaves

1/2 head garlic, with cloves peeled

1/2 cup canned tomato purée

5 whole black peppercorns

**YIELD: About 2 1/2 quarts**

*A nice venison stock can be made in the same way by substituting venison bones for the veal or beef bones.*

Preheat the oven to 450°F.

Place the bones in a roasting pan, sprinkle them with salt and roast until brown, at least 30 minutes.

Remove the bones from the oven and place them and the water, along with all the other ingredients, in a stockpot over high heat. After the liquid comes to a boil, lower the heat so the liquid simmers gently. (Do not allow the stock to boil rapidly, or it will turn cloudy.) Cook the stock, partially covered, skimming occasionally to remove foam and solids, for 2 to 3 hours. When the stock is done, strain it into a large bowl through a colander lined with cheesecloth or a fine sieve.

Return the strained stock to the pot and cook over high heat until it is reduced to 1/3 of its volume.

## Glace de Viande with Veal

2 pounds raw veal or beef bones

3 tablespoons salt

8 quarts water

2 2/3 cups sliced yellow onions

2 cups sliced carrots

1 cup sliced leeks

1 2/3 cups sliced celery

1 cup chopped flat leaf parsley

1 teaspoon dried thyme

2 whole bay leaves

1/2 head garlic, with cloves peeled

1/2 cup canned tomato purée

5 whole black peppercorns

**YIELD: 4 to 6 servings**

Bring 2 cups of veal stock (see the previous recipe) to a boil, then reduce the heat so it simmers briskly. Continue simmering until the stock is reduced to about 1/2 cup of syrupy liquid.

## Red Horseradish Cocktail Sauce

1 cup ketchup

2 tablespoons prepared horseradish

1/8 teaspoon Louisiana-style hot sauce

juice of 1/2 lemon

dash worchestershire sauce

**YIELD: 1 1/2 cups**

Combine all ingredients in a bowl with a whisk and chill until serving time.

## White Horseradish Sauce

2 tablespoons prepared horseradish

1 tablespoon cider vinegar

1 teaspoon dry mustard

3 tablespoons mayonnaise

1/8 teaspoon ground red pepper

1/2 cup sour cream

**YIELD: 1 1/2 cups**

In a large bowl, fold the horseradish, salt and pepper into the sour cream. Refrigerate for at least 1 hour before serving, for the flavors to blend.

## Mignonette Sauce

1 French shallot, finely chopped

1/2 cup dry white wine

1 tablespoon sherry vinegar

white peppper, to taste

salt, to taste

1 tablespoon finely chopped parsley or green onion

**YIELD: 1/2 cup**

Combine all ingredients in a bowl with a whisk and chill until serving time.

## Clarified Butter

1 pound unsalted butter

*Whole butter is a blend of fat, milk solids and water. Clarified butter, also called drawn butter, is simply the butterfat obtained by separating it from the solids and water. This clear golden liquid often performs as a sinfully delicious dip for cooked artichoke leaves, lobster and other shellfish.*

*Cooks prefer clarified to whole butter for sautéeing or pan-frying because it has a higher smoke point, meaning that, at higher temperatures, it doesn't burn as quickly as whole butter does.*

*Occasionally, both whole and clarified butters are used in the same recipe. Similarly, clarified butter and another fat, such as olive oil, are sometimes used together in a dish.*

*This recipe can be multiplied or divided.*

**YIELD: 1 1/2 cups**

In a heavy, 2-quart saucepan, heat the butter over medium-high heat just until melted. Reduce the heat to low and continue cooking about two minutes until a layer of clear golden liquid (which is the clarified butter or butterfat) has developed between the foam on top and the milk solids and milky water that have separated from the butter and sunken to the bottom of the pan.

Remove the pan from the heat, and skim and discard the foam on top. Ladle the clarified butter into a clean pan or large glass measuring cup, being careful not to include any of the milk solids and water as you work. Discard the milk solids and water.

Use the clarified butter immediately or let it cool briefly, then store it in an airtight container in the refrigerator for later use. It will last up to one month.

## Garlic Butter

3/4 pound (3 sticks) unsalted butter, softened

1 cup chopped flat-leaf parsley

1/4 cup Herbsaint or other anisette liqueur such as Pernod

2 tablespoons finely chopped garlic

salt and freshly ground pepper, to taste

**YIELD: 1 1/2 cups**

Allow the butter to soften. In an electric mixer or food processor, mix the butter until it is smooth. Add the chopped garlic and process until smooth, then add the Herbsaint, chopped parsley, and salt and pepper to taste.

Mix until completely smooth and all the liqueur has been absorbed. This may take 3 to 5 minutes in an electric mixer, but will take less time in a food processor. Taste for seasoning and adjust if necessary.

## Lemon Butter

12 tablespoons (1 1/2 sticks) unsalted butter

juice of 1 lemon

salt and freshly ground white pepper, to taste

2 teaspoons chopped Italian (flat leaf) parsley

**YIELD: 1 cup**

*Nothing simpler or more sensational.*

Melt the butter in a saucepan over medium heat and then add the lemon juice. Season to taste with salt and white pepper and stir in the parsley. Remove from heat and keep warm until needed.

# Sauces

## Bordelaise Sauce

2 tablespoons unsalted butter

1/4 cup minced shallots

1 cup dry red wine

1 bouquet garni (page 219)

1 whole clove

1 black peppercorn

1/2 clove garlic

1 whole bay leaf

1 quart veal stock (page 212)

1 tablespoon glace de viande or
veal demi-glace (page 212)

salt and freshly ground black pepper, to taste

**YIELD: about 2 cups**

Melt the butter in a small pan over medium heat. When the foam has subsided, add the shallots and sauté until soft, about 5 minutes. Add the red wine, increase the heat to medium-high and bring to a boil.

Add the bouquet garni, clove, peppercorn, garlic, bay leaf and veal stock. Bring up to a boil, then reduce the heat to very low, and simmer until the volume is reduced by about half and the sauce coats the back of a spoon. Stir in the glacé de viande, season to taste with salt and pepper, and strain into a clean pan.

If desired, cool the sauce to room temperature, then refrigerate it in an airtight container. At serving time, warm the sauce in the top of a double boiler over gently simmering water, stirring.

## Beurre Blanc

1/4 cup white wine

1 tablespoon very finely chopped French shallots or white parts only of green onions

1/4 cup heavy cream

8 tablespoons (1 stick) unsalted butter, cut into 8 chunks

1 tablespoon lemon juice

**YIELD: 1 cup**

In a small saucepan, combine the wine, cream and shallot and place over medium-high heat. Bring to a boil, then reduce the heat to low. Simmer gently, watching carefully, for about 10 minutes, or until the liquid is reduced to about 2 tablespoons.

(At this point, the wine-and-cream mixture can be set aside for up to 1 hour before the remainder of the recipe is completed.)

If the wine-and cream mixture has been prepared ahead, place the saucepan over low heat to warm through, if necessary.

As soon as the liquid is steaming, add all the butter at once and swirl the pan or whisk the mixture continuously until the butter has been thoroughly absorbed and the consistency is smooth. Remove from heat immediately.

Quickly stir in the pepper and chives. Use within 10 minutes or keep warm, covered, in the top of a double boiler over hot but not simmering water for up to 1 hour, stirring occasionally.

## Hollandaise Sauce

3 tablespoons water

3 large egg yolks

salt and freshly ground white pepper, to taste

ice cubes, if needed

1/2 cup warm (not hot) clarified butter (page 214)

2 to 3 teaspoons fresh lemon juice, or as needed

**YIELD: 1 1/4 cups**

*Adding the lemon juice at the very end makes the freshest-tasting hollandaise.*

In a small, heavy saucepan, combine the water, egg yolks and a pinch of salt. Whisk constantly over low heat until the mixture is foamy and thick enough to form a ribbon when the whisk is pulled from the mixture. It should be pale yellow with the consistency of a thin yogurt.

(This stage is crucial: Once the mixture has thickened, if it continues to heat it will curdle. This is the technique for saving the sauce: Be ready to pull the saucepan off the heat and have an ice cube or two on hand. If the mixture goes beyond the thick and creamy stage and appears even a little bit granular, quickly drop an ice cube into the mixture and whisk it in.)

When the mixture has reached the correct foamy consistency, cool the pan by tipping it to the side and carefully holding the base of the pan under cold running water for a few seconds. This will stop the sauce from cooking any further.

Off the heat, begin adding the warm (not hot) clarified butter drop by drop, whisking all the time. Add the butter very slowly for about 30 seconds, then add the rest of the butter in a very thin, steady stream, whisking until it is all incorporated.

Whisk in 2 teaspoons of lemon juice and taste. You should be able to taste the lemon, but it should not overpower the delicate sauce or taste sour. Add more lemon juice bit by bit, if necessary, to achieve the perfect balance. Adjust the seasoning with salt and add a pinch of white pepper. Serve immediately or hold in the top of a double-boiler over hot, but not simmering or boiling, water for up to 45 minutes.

## Blender Hollandaise

4 tablespoons (1 stick) unsalted butter

3 large egg yolks

2 tablespoons fresh lemon juice

1/4 teaspoon salt

dash of freshly ground white pepper

**YIELD: 3/4 cup**

*If mastering the classic preparation of hollandaise sauce is too much to contemplate, we offer this alternative that is foolproof and quite tasty.*

Over medium heat in a small saucepan, heat the butter until it melts. Remove from the heat and immediately place the egg yolks, lemon juice, salt and pepper in a blender.

Cover and blend at medium speed for about 5 seconds. Reduce the blender speed to low and slowly add the hot melted butter through the opening in the cover. When all the butter has been incorporated, switch to high speed for 30 seconds.

Serve immediately or hold in the top of a double-boiler over hot, but not simmering or boiling, water for up to 45 minutes.

## Béchamel Sauce

1/3 cup (about 5 1/2 tablespoons) unsalted butter

1/3 cup all-purpose flour

2 cups whole milk

1/2 cup sliced white onion

1 bouquet garni (page 219)

1 clove

1 whole bay leaf

salt and freshly ground white pepper, to taste

**YIELD: about 2 1/2 cups**

Prepare a white roux by first melting the butter in a saucepan over low heat. Stir in the flour 1 teaspoon at a time to form a paste. When the paste begins to foam gently, stir for a minute or two without browning, to cook off the raw taste of the flour. Remove from the heat.

In a saucepan over medium-high heat, combine the milk, onion, bouquet garni, clove and bay leaf and bring to a boil. Reduce the heat so the milk is simmering. Gradually add the roux, whisking in 1 tablespoon at a time, then simmer for a minute or two, until it reaches a consistency that will coat the back of a spoon. Whisk in the salt and white pepper.

## White Wine Sauce

2 teaspoons unsalted butter

1 tablespoon chopped French shallot

1 whole bay leaf

1 teaspoon whole peppercorns

3/4 cup dry white wine

1 1/2 cups fish stock (preferred ) or chicken stock

1 1/2 cups heavy cream

1 tablespoon cornstarch

2 tablespoons cold water

**YIELD: 2 cups**

In a saucepan over medium heat, melt the butter and sauté the shallots until transparent, about 5 minutes. Add the bay leaf and peppercorns and sauté for 1 minute. Stir in the white wine, stock and cream. Increase the heat to moderate and simmer the sauce, stirring frequently, until reduced by about half.

Make a slurry by dissolving the cornstarch in the cold water and add it slowly to the sauce, stirring all the time. Return the liquid to a simmer and stir for 3 minutes to allow the cornstarch to thicken the sauce and lose its raw taste. Strain through a sieve to remove peppercorns and bay leaf and use immediately or, if desired, cool, cover and refrigerate for up to 3 days.

# Seasonings

*Many chefs, wishing to control recipe consistency, measure and mix their own spices and herbs in advance. Some of them have packaged them and created successful businesses.*

*New Orleanians have always known about seasoning blends. We take great delight in creating our personal batches of seasoned items including flours, oils, vinegars butters, and herb and spice mixtures. These are all easily purchased but it is much more satisfying to prepare one's own.*

*It is best to prepare seasoning blends without salt, balancing the sodium levels of the actual dish based on other ingredients (for the same reason that unsalted butter is generally preferred for cooking).*

*The method is to prepare small batches and store them in tightly covered containers, since dried herbs lose their intensity over time. The colorful jars make excellent gifts.*

## Seafood Seasoning

2 tablespoons granulated garlic

2 tablespoons granulated onion

2 tablespoons freshly ground black pepper

1 teaspoon powdered oregano

1/2 teaspoon powdered thyme

1/2 teaspoon freshly ground white pepper

1/4 teaspoon powdered basil

1/4 teaspoon cayenne pepper

**YIELD: about 1/2 cup**

Mix all ingredients together using a fork or place in a jar, cover and shake it thoroughly. Store in tightly covered container.

## Seasoned Flour

1/2 cup all-purpose flour

1/4 cup corn flour

1 tablespoon cornstarch

1 tablespoon salt

1 tablespoon paprika

1 teaspoon onion powder

1 teaspoon freshly ground black pepper

1/2 teaspoon garlic powder

1/4 teaspoon cayenne pepper

*Seasoned flour is a basic staple in a New Orleans pantry. It is always on hand to coat seafood and meats for frying or sautéeing, or boosting the flavor of some savory dish that calls for all-purpose flour.*

**YIELD: 1 cup**

Thoroughly combine all the ingredients in a small mixing bowl.

The seasoned flour can be stored in an airtight container in a refrigerator or other cool, dark place for up to 3 months.

## Creole Seasoning

3 tablespoons sweet paprika

2 tablespoons onion powder

2 tablespoons garlic powder

2 tablespoons dried oregano leaves

2 tablespoons dried sweet basil

1 tablespoon dried thyme leaves

1 tablespoon freshly ground black pepper

1 tablespoon freshly ground white pepper

1 tablespoon cayenne pepper

1 tablespoon salt

Dash of chili powder

Dash of cumin powder

**YIELD: about 1/2 cup**

NOTE: For blackened seasoning, add an additional tablespoon each of paprika and cayenne pepper for color and heat.

Mix all ingredients together using a fork or place in a jar, cover and shake it thoroughly. Store in tightly covered container.

## Fresh Bouquet Garni

1/2 bunch parsley

3 whole bay leaves

1 sprig fresh thyme

1 celery stalk celery, including tops, chopped

**YIELD: 3/4 cup**

*Bouquet garni is the French term for a bundle of fresh herbs tied together and tossed into the pot. It is then removed so the seasonings do not remain in the dish.*

Place the fresh herbs and celery in the center of a 7-inch square of cheesecloth. Draw the four corners of the cheesecloth together at the top and tie the corners together to form a small pouch; or, use a tea ball if the quantity is small enough. Add the bouquet garni to the dish being prepared, then, when the dish is cooked, fish it out with a slotted spoon and discard.

## Dry Bouquet Garni

4 cloves

1 whole bay leaf

1 teaspoon black peppercorns

1 teaspoon dried thyme

1/2 teaspoon dried marjoram

**YIELD: 3/4 cup**

Place the dried herbs and spices in the center of a 7-inch square of cheesecloth. Draw the four corners of the cheesecloth together at the top and tie the corners together to form a small pouch; or, use a tea ball if the quantity is small enough. Add the bouquet garni to the dish being prepared, then, when the dish is cooked, fish it out with a slotted spoon and discard.

# Acknowledgements

We'd like to thank the many dedicated oyster farmers, restaurateurs and chefs who have provided their unrelenting commitment to quality and their loyalty to our families since P&J Oyster Company was founded in 1876. With all our hearts we thank you.

We appreciate greatly the dedication of the oyster shuckers, delivery drivers and the scores of others who work alongside us day in and day out. You help us to provide our customers with the quality that defines P&J oysters. We are grateful for your loyalty, hard work and perseverance.

We are grateful also to Kit Wohl for bringing to reality a cookbook that reflects Mama's culinary spirit and high standards.

We're always happy to hear from our friends. Simply e-mail us at info@oysterlover.com or click in at www.oysterlover.com.

To everyone, merci bien!

*~ Al Sunseri, Sal Sunseri, Merri Sunseri Schneider and Blake Sunseri*


Our thanks to the Sunseri family for entrusting their mother's vision to us.

A toast to our well-fed testing assistants, Chris Gromek, Zachary Engel and Elouisa Rivera. Chefs Robert Barker and Shane Baird provided their expertise and editor Gene Bourg lent his skills, humor and organization. Michael Lauve did his creative magic.

Farewell to a cherished friend, the late Archie A. Casbarian, an amazing restaurateur, who set me on this path with Arnaud's Restaurant Cookbook.

Most of all, great love and appreciation for Billy, my extraordinary husband. Please visit us at www.kitwohl.com or e-mail kit@kitwohl.com.

*~ Kit Wohl*